The ANIMAL REVIEW

The ANIMAL
REVIEW

The Genius, Mediocrity, and Breathtaking
Stupidity That Is Nature

JACOB LENTZ *and* **STEVE NASH**

New York Berlin London

Published by Bloomsbury USA, New York

All papers used by Bloomsbury USA are natural, recyclable products made from wood grown in well-managed forests. The manufacturing processes conform to the environmental regulations of the country of origin.

Stock photo credits:

Corbis: p. 19 © Bettmann/Corbis; p. 42 © Image Source/Corbis; p. 74 © Denis Scott/Corbis; p. 83 © Norbert Wu/Science Faction/Corbis

Getty Images: p. 9

iStockphoto: pp. 2, 5, 12, 13, 16–18, 20, 23, 24, 25, 27, 30–31, 33, 34, 35, 38, 40–41, 43, 44, 48, 50, 51, 52, 53, 55, 57, 58, 59, 65, 66, 69, 71, 77, 78, 80, 81, 90, 91, 92, 97, 98, 101, 104, 105, 111, 112, 119, 120, 122, 124, 127, 128

Oceanlight: pp. 75 and 86 © Phillip Colla Natural History Photography

SeaPics: pp. 84 and 85

Shutterstock: pp. 7, 8, 11, 36, 49, 60, 67, 76, 79, 95, 99, 106, 121

LIBRARY OF CONGRESS CATALOGING-IN-PUBLICATION DATA HAS BEEN APPLIED FOR.

ISBN: 978-1-60819-025-6

First U.S. edition 2010

1 3 5 7 9 10 8 6 4 2

Designed by Elizabeth Van Itallie
Printed and bound in China by Hung Hing Offset Printing Company Ltd.

FOR DAVID WEINSTEIN

CONTENTS

Foreword. viii

LAND 1

Panda. 2
King Cobra 4
Wildebeest 7
Garden Snail 11
Spotlight on Poisonous Snakes 15
Giraffe 16
North American Mountain Goat. 19
Bullet Ant. 24
Spotlight on Bears 30
Alpaca 32
Koala 36
Spotlight on Apes. 40
Skunk. 42

SKY 47

Bald Eagle. 48
Locust 53
Owl 57
Spotlight on Birding. 60
Vulture. 62
Pigeon 67

WATER

WATER 73
Blue Whale 74
Great White Shark 78
Swordfish 83
Sea Cucumber 86
Spotlight on Extinction 89
Sponge 90
Clam 91
Spotlight on Taxonomy 95
Salmon 97
Octopus 103

OTHER 109
Hippopotamus 110
Golden Dart Frog 115
Peacock 119
Spotlight on Animal Sounds 123
Capybara 124
Ladybug 127

Photography/Art Credits 132
Acknowledgments 133

FOREWORD

Early Man lacked biology textbooks. And so, after first laying eyes on a woolly mammoth, his "scientific" assessment was limited to:

1) That hairy thing is very big.
2) I bet there's enough meat on there to last, like, forever.
3) I wonder if anyone else knows about this.

Of course, there were other important things to learn about woolly mammoths—their five-meter tusks, for instance—but again, Early Man wasn't exactly winning any science fairs and eventually decided to drop out of school to pursue a failed career as a cave artist anyway. But science marched on. At some point during the so-called "Enlightenment," the study of the natural world took on a nonjudgmental bent, and while this may have allowed for clearer discussions between scientists, it ignored the fundamental reality that some parts of Nature are more interesting than others. Nowhere is this truer than in Kingdom Animalia. Is anyone really going to argue that a sponge is as interesting as a parrot? And if anyone is, can someone please pull that person aside for a talking-to? Because that's just insane.

Moreover, why bother to figure out how the universe works if not then to declare that the ways it works are often stupid? No more. Herein you will find zoology as it was meant to be presented: as subjective judgment. Within this book you will find various animals discussed, reviewed, and graded on their merits as the facts dictate. The scientific information in here is true, and the opinions rendered are true as well. We've done a lot of thinking about these animals, and we're pretty sure that we've gotten them all graded fairly and sans prejudice.

Many scientists would prefer that others not use their research to issue grades, both for ethical reasons and because they don't see the fun in it. But many scientists also use binomial nomenclature and words like *phylum* and *genera*, which shows the kind of things scientists consider fun. For our part, we've come up with a much simpler classification system for the animal kingdom, and we're using it for the first time in this book. Instead of getting into the confusions of orders and classes, et cetera, we've divided up animals into much simpler categories: Land, Sky, Water, and Other. Land includes land animals. Sky includes sky animals. Water includes water animals. Other includes species that can't make up their minds between them.

See how simple that is?

We wish you a wonderful reading experience.

Best of luck,
Jake and Steve

P.S. By the way, please try not to feel too bad for the animals that don't get the grade you think they should. The reality is that, no matter how much you might love them, most of them secretly hold you in contempt, and they're usually lying when they tell you that they couldn't call you back because their cell phone died. Their cell phone works fine. Trust us.

P.P.S. We still use the scientific classification of animals where necessary as a good-faith gesture that we mean science no harm.

LAND

PANDA

After toys with lead in them, food products with lead in them, and lead toys with food in them, pandas (*Ailuropoda melanoleuca*, lit. "black-and-white black cat foot bear who suffers depression") are China's fourth-biggest export. They are best known for sitting dumbly in zoos around the world while visitors fawn over them and their adorable Chinese names. While about sixteen hundred pandas are alive in the wild, the vast majority (about thirty-two) live in foreign zoos, where most of their time is dedicated to not mating. There are also some pandas in Chinese zoos, which makes as much sense as opening a Taco Bell in the middle of Mexico City: You'll get a few tourists, but the locals know where the authentic, non-mass-produced food (pandas) is (are).

Much ado is made about the plight of the panda. Pandas are endangered due to habitat destruction, the Chinese tradition of poaching, and a hilariously low birth rate. While their exact fertility rates are unknown (it's kind of a personal question), most experts believe

"Guess what I won't be doing anytime soon."

that pandas reproduce once every ten million years. This has prompted aggressive captivity-breeding programs. These never work, because getting pandas to mate is like launching a satellite into orbit. Simply put, pandas and mating are like Quakers and military drafts. Zookeepers have even resorted to showing them pornography, which is more a measure of desperation than scientific training.

Every so often captive pandas *will* mate (always by accident), and the local news then runs endless loops of a gross panda cub in an incubator as it plots a life of not mating.

Pandas' problems come from their basic refusal to act like real bears. First of all, real bears like to mate. Real bears also eat things they're supposed to eat. But pandas, despite having the digestive tract of a carnivore that cannot effectively digest cellulose, nevertheless insist on keeping to a diet that is 90 percent bamboo. This means that they have to feed constantly, subtracting from time that could otherwise be spent at least pretending to care about mating.

While everyone worries about the panda's future, any objective observer is led to the conclusion that perhaps its time has passed. Maybe Nature is trying to give them the hint that they need to go the way of the dodo, and maybe we should spend our time on a species that at least *wants* to survive. In the meantime, pandas occupy valuable zoo space and consume prodigious amounts of bamboo that could otherwise be used to produce offbeat furniture. Way to be, Gao Gao.

In conclusion, pandas are literally a dying breed, and whatever their charms or ability to symbolize goodwill between us and a Communist regime, the species leaves a great deal to be desired.

GRADE: F

FUN FACT The number of species on earth (including animals, microbes, fungi, everything) is estimated to be somewhere between two and one hundred million. You probably stepped on a few hundred thousand just this morning.

KING COBRA

Let's begin by giving King Cobra its final grade: A+.

There are two reasons for this: 1) This is the single most obvious grade to be given out for anything ever in the history of grades being given out for things, and 2) Like you're going to be the person who gives King Cobra an A-. Yeah, good luck with that one.

For most other animals, it would define absurdity to dispense a grade prior to the actual review, but then again, most animals aren't King Cobra. And that, friends, is very good news for everyone. Because if most animals were King Cobra, the animals that *weren't* King Cobra would soon be dead from fright. And venom.

Granted, King Cobra is not the single most venomous snake in the world,[1] but it's better not to bring this up in the company of King Cobra. One bite from King Cobra is enough to kill twenty-five people or drop an elephant. Sometimes King Cobra does this as a party trick.

King Cobra's other party trick is to raise up to one third of its body off the ground and scare the living hell out of everyone at the party. Being the world's longest venomous snake, and having been recorded in the wild at up to eighteen and a half feet, King Cobra can raise himself up high enough to look a full-grown man in the eye. King Cobra will then let out a bone-chilling hiss that sounds something like a growling dog. King Cobra has ruined many a party with his so-called "tricks."

But please don't anyone tell King Cobra that nobody likes his

---

[1] This is actually fairly difficult to determine definitively, because one must consider the toxicity of said venom (which is either a neuro- or hemotoxin or both, and is always a polypeptide), the amount of venom the snake carries (King Cobra carries a ton because King Cobra is so massive), and a snake's relative aggressiveness. Still, the late, great Steve Irwin did a special on the world's deadliest snakes (six of which are in Australia, so, you know, don't go *there*) and pronounced the Fierce Snake (Australia, of course) the deadliest. That said, it's really up to the individual animal to decide whose deadly venom they want to get bitten with.

"HEY, WHAT'S UP?"

party tricks. That dude gets weird.

By calling itself King Cobra, King Cobra was making a bold statement, but bolder still is King Cobra's Latinate name, *Ophiophagus hannah*, which literally means "snake eater." King Cobra picked it during first-year Latin class to let the other snakes know what's up, and it's working so far. King Cobra's diet consists of other snakes, including large pythons and, yes, smaller King Cobras. To say that King Cobra has an "appetite for destruction" is not just a terrible play on words—it's also deadly accurate (thanks to neurotoxic venom).

King Cobra does what King Cobra wants, when King Cobra wants. Like building nests. King Cobra is the only snake known to build nests for its eggs. King Cobra also likes to dance to flutes. And to shed its skin wherever it wants and leave it there as a reminder: "King Cobra was here."

If anyone ever tells you that maybe King Cobra is trying to overcompensate for a complete lack of appendages, stay away from that person. You don't want King Cobra lumping you in with them if that gets around.

King Cobra is currently working on time travel and invisibility.

GRADE: A+

WILDEBEEST

Part ox, part horse, and entirely traumatized, the wildebeest (genus *Connochaetes*, lit. "hamburger of the Serengeti") is welcomed to Animal Review. Please say hello—and probably goodbye while you're at it—as it's unlikely the wildebeest will make it to the end of this review alive.

Rare photo of a wildebeest not being disemboweled.

As you've no doubt noticed on the Discovery Channel, the wildebeest is Nature's punching bag. It pretty much exists as a proving ground for the weapons of evolution. Indeed, the wildebeest spends the majority of its time testing the efficacy of teeth, claws, beaks, maws, and neurotoxic venoms for an impressive roster of high-profile clientele on the African continent. But it's a living, and the wildebeest makes the most of it. As far as being willing to take collective hits repeatedly and still get up and go to work the next day, this animal is second to none. Boston-based defense contractor Raytheon

Actual passport picture of a wildebeest.

would do well to consider the wildebeest for upcoming trials of the next-generation Tomahawk cruise missiles. They probably wouldn't mind.

If wildebeests have any philosophy, it's definitely safety in numbers. They're always running around in herds, literally stepping over each other to avoid a macabre tragedy at some murky river's edge. Their social arrangements are akin to those of freshman nerds who hang together in the back of the lunchroom, gripped with relentless terror that a jock (lion) will pick on (eat) them.

Wildebeests, of course, are also famous for their enormous seasonal migration, during which more than one million animals leave the Serengeti in search of more dry grass to eat somewhere else. The migration is their Memorial Day weekend, except in this case they play the roles of both the cars on the freeway *and* the meat on the barbecues.

Whilst the migration may not always bring good fortune to the wildebeest, it does serve a relatively useful purpose for Mother Earth. One million wildebeests charging out of the Serengeti and making

moving pit stops along the way is essentially a giant conveyer belt of fertilizer. They tramp down the grass, add some nitrogen-rich nutrients to the soil, and presto: a nice new lawn for Africa. Plus, their ever-present rotting carcasses add that certain *je ne sais quoi* to the ecology of the grassland. Say what you will about wildebeests, they take this recycling stuff seriously.

Moreover, just because the life expectancy of a wildebeest is a few hours doesn't mean that we should dismiss it lightly. They have an important, tragic job (feeding pretty much everyone), and they do it with grace and aplomb. And as with the nerds in high school, there's at least a moderate chance that we'll all end up working for them someday.

GRADE: B

FUN FACT Some gazelles and an antelope called the springbok perform a seemingly risky jumping display called pronking (aka pronging or stotting) when pursued by a predator. Because pronking slows the animal down but looks impressive, scientists believe it might be a form of showing off, as if to say to the predator, "Behold my agility. Chasing me is a waste of your time. Maybe try Todd over there with the runny nose and the scientific calculator who can't pronk to save his life. Seriously, you should go kill Todd."

GARDEN SNAIL

The garden snail (*Helix aspersa*, lit. "three-dimensional corkscrew-shaped appetizer") is a terrestrial mollusk that never really figured out how to get positive results from Evolution. In defense of the snail, that's not an easy task, because Evolution is a manic-depressive genius and famously difficult to work with on *anything*. Plus the garden snail seems to keep catching Evolution in its "experimental" periods.

Apparently Evolution just broke up with its girlfriend.

When confronted by the same complicated problems, epoch after epoch, Evolution produces a host of different solutions. (There are about nine unique plans for the eye, for example, each designed when Evolution went off its meds.) These tend to range from the breathtaking to the absurd (again, depending on Evolution's mood at the time). Unfortunately for *H. aspersa*, Evolution was on what it was certain was a creative (though also quite likely chemically influenced) high when it decided to make the garden snail's Big Three—Sensory Organs, Locomotion, and Reproduction—and the result of its three-day all-nighter was somehow at once both far too much and yet not nearly enough.

Here's a tip: When Evolution suddenly gets up, locks itself in the bathroom, and turns on the shower so you can't hear it sobbing in Latin, that's not the time to stand in the eye line—at least not if you're hoping for complex, autofocusing, mammalian eyes with a large dynamic contrast ratio and a nice, roomy, dedicated visual cortex for data processing. However, if you *are* in the eye line at that point, you could end up with light-sensitive eyestalks that Evolution purchased from Wal-Mart and keeps referring to as "found art" and his "latest masterpiece."

"SAY . . . YOU DIDN'T KEEP THE RECEIPT BY ANY CHANCE?"

Complementing its flimsy, cheap, light-sensing "eyes" (assembly required, batteries not included, online pdf manual impossible to find and poorly translated[1]), Evolution then decided to dedicate *H. aspersa*'s remaining two face-based tentacles to touch and smell, though precisely why is anyone's guess. As pleased as Evolution was with this creative choice, the design ended up a case study on the dangers of placing too much faith in one's genius, as the typical snail just ends up confused over which of the four tentacles to use in

---

[1] The English version of the garden snail's online light-sensing-eyestalk manual instructs it to "Insert Cornea tab A1 into Retina slot B3 and take 16mm screw please include to fassen [*sic*] to Optic Nerve." And then for no clear reason it switches to German. What a mess.

which situation, and it's not infrequent that these animals stick an eye into a carton of milk to smell if it's gone bad. To paraphrase the words of Evolution's former business manager, it's just too much for no reason at all.

Locomotion in the snail begat another moment of creative turpitude for Evolution. Bored with what it kept lambasting as "pedestrian" modes of transit, such as walking, Evolution gave snails what seems to be some kind of deeply ironic commentary about some social issue that none of us will ever really understand. Anyway, whatever Evolution's bigger point is here, snails are left to get around town by sliding their single "foot" over a trail of their own mucus, meaning that the garden snail tops out around .03 mph at full throttle with snot boosters set to max. Suffice it to say, this marked the low point for Evolution's career, as even the Arts section of the *New York Times* offered only measured praise, prompting Evolution to cancel its subscription for two weeks and causing a minor sensation around Manhattan that ended only when the newspaper's ombudsman wrote an apology.

"Anyone wanna swap for a pair of legs? Don't bother answering—I'm also deaf."

A complete creative nadir was reached with Evolution's indefensible choices for the garden snail for sexual reproduction. First of all, it made all of them hermaphrodites, but that wasn't "new" enough, apparently. When two garden snails contemplate reproduction, one of them initiates the act by injecting the other with a mystery mucus (of course) using what scientists call a "love dart." After the unveiling of the love dart to a capacity crowd at its gallery, Evolution noticed that most of the spectators were either confusedly staring at said love dart and/or quietly picking at their hors d'oeuvres. After a long, uncomfortable pause and some polite clapping, someone had the temerity to ask if the love dart was a metaphor for a collectivized Oedipus complex. Well, everyone got the answer to *that* question when Evolution threw its champagne in the questioner's face and stomped out of the room.

It was a long time before answers could be had, as soon thereafter Evolution stopped giving interviews. But in March of 2006, some researchers at Canada's famed McGill University in Montreal did an experiment in which they cut off some snails' love darts[2] and proceeded to inject one group with saltwater and the other with the mystery mucus. They found that the mystery mucus delivered by the love darts actually doubles a snail's potential to produce offspring. In short, Evolution wasn't completely off—just mostly. And in point of fact, it also turns out that snail researchers double their chances of *not* mating simply by performing snail research.

Snails are, in short, a mess. They're tragically underwhelming in their complexity, and they make clear that even the best natural selectors make bad choices. And since nobody else seems willing to say it: Sorry, Evolution—you screwed up on this one.

GRADE: D-

---

[2] It's cool—they grow back.

SPOTLIGHT ON:
POISONOUS SNAKES

People spend a huge amount of time debating which venomous snake is the deadliest. It's not all cut and dry (see King Cobra) because one's definition of deadliosity has to factor in venom type and mechanism of action, amount delivered per bite, the snake's aggressiveness, and frequency of contact with humans. Ranking them, then, becomes quite difficult. Besides, as is often said, the deadliest venomous snake is the one that just bit you.

Here, then, is the gist of what you need to know about venomous snakes.

- There are lots and lots of them, especially in Africa, Asia, and Australia (extra-especially in Australia, where venomous snakes are so populous that a king brown snake once served as an MP from Canberra).
- Most of them can kill you. All the ones in Australia can kill you.
- Avoid them at all costs.
- Don't sleep or walk in high brush (in Australia).
- Don't climb trees if you don't know what's up there (in Australia).
- Don't climb around under fallen eucalyptus trees in Australia or inside Australian crevices, or under Australian houses.
- Don't go to Australia.
- Don't befriend Australian tourists (they may have snakes in their luggage).
- Don't listen to Men at Work.
- Don't go to Hugh Jackman movies.
- Don't ever let Nicole Kidman come over to your house for dinner. Unless you want to make friendly dinner conversation with her deadly inland taipan. (They're less interesting than you think, and belligerent drunks to boot.)

That is all.

GIRAFFE

The giraffe (*Giraffa camelopardalis*, lit. "tiny, but said ironically") is Nature's concept car. Large and impractical, the giraffe was never meant for mass production, but some executive fell in love with it at Detroit's Annual Animal Trade Show a few years back, and giraffes have been losing money ever since.

Massive ungulates and the tallest of the land animals, giraffes can be up to eighteen feet high and thirty-eight hundred pounds, and most of that is neck. Like most mammals, the neck of a giraffe has seven vertebrae, though in the giraffe each of them is elongated and covered in tacky chrome plating. Looking to justify the expense, the neck was put to use for getting leaves off acacia trees on the African plains, which was sold in the giraffe marketing campaign with the slogan *Whether in the Whole Foods produce aisle or on the Serengeti Plain—you'll never go hungry.* And then, in a truly gauche finishing touch, the giraffe's head was topped with two ridiculous-looking cartilage horns.

"Let's throw some horns on it. There we go. Now that says class."

Unsurprisingly, the enormity of the giraffe created more problems than it was worth. To move blood against gravity up the neck, a giraffe requires a two-foot-diameter heart. It requires special anchor muscles to keep the neck upright. It requires a complex pressure-regulation system in the upper neck to prevent blood overflow to the brain when the giraffe bends over to fill up. And it requires a tight sheath of thick skin over its legs to keep the capillaries from bursting due to all that blood being pulled down by gravity from such unnecessary heights. All this requires energy. Too bad, acacia trees.

"Forget the stupid laws of physics! Let's make this one BIG!"

As one might suspect, the giraffe's size isn't the advantage the guy at the dealership says it is. Sure, giraffes can eat from trees, and most predators leave them alone, but it's not uncommon for lions to give a go at knocking a giraffe off its feet. Then these very same lions will promptly eat the giraffe. As a rule of thumb, once one thing goes wrong with your giraffe, several other things are likely to follow. Repairs are famously expensive, and a certified giraffe mechanic can sometimes clear six figures a year.

"What do you mean 'trunk space'? Are you high?"

Since giraffe necks are, in the end, status symbols, male giraffes naturally use them to fight with each other. Because what else are they gonna do? Leg wrestle? No, they are not going to leg wrestle. They need their legs to try to get away from lions.

So conceptual is the giraffe design that each individual giraffe has a unique pattern of spots, adding further pointless costs out of the factory. Originally meant to appeal to collectors, it's yet to catch on in the classic land-mammal community and has provided an easy way for lions to coordinate among themselves *which* giraffe they're going to knock off its feet and then eat.

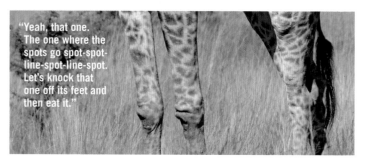

"Yeah, that one. The one where the spots go spot-spot-line-spot-line-spot. Let's knock that one off its feet and then eat it."

The one feature of the giraffe that might stand the test of time is its insomnia: A giraffe requires just ten minutes to two hours of sleep per day. The rest of the time is spent up on blocks in your friend's dad's garage, where nothing on it ever gets fixed but he keeps telling everyone not to go near it.

GRADE: D

FUN FACT A rhinoceros's horn is made of keratin, the same protein in human hair, though it's much more useful for stabbing and gouging than human hair.

NORTH AMERICAN MOUNTAIN GOAT

The very first thing you learn in a veterinary comparative-anatomy course is that animals indigenous to North America are pretty lame compared to their counterparts in the rest of the world. That's not to say that animals such as rattlesnakes and bobcats are boring per se. But compare a bobcat to a Siberian tiger or place a rattler side by side with a King Cobra (n.b.: You will instantly regret doing this), and you're left with the inescapable conclusion that many North American fauna are rapidly falling behind.

Let's face facts. Our eagles are bald, our trout are swimming at third-grade levels, the star-nosed mole is an unmitigated disaster, and, with the extinction of the American mastodon, 100 percent of our circus elephants are now imported from overseas. And to think North America was once home to the Tyrannosaurus rex. These

The Pacific Northwest's grainy, eighteen-frames-per-second Bigfoot vs. Nepal's laser-eyed (apparently) Yeti? Game over.

days it's become so bad that even our pretend animals are clearly outmatched.

But all is not lost. North America has a shining hero of an exception in the Goat Division: the North American mountain goat (*Oreamnos americanus*, lit. "mountain goat American"). A large, sure-footed, attractive, aggressive, even-toed ungulate, the North American mountain goat manages to at least achieve parity with high-altitude goats across the globe. Even its harshest international rivals, when pressed, will admit it's rather cool.

"Any of you camels, koalas, or snow monkeys wanna climb up here and try to knock me off? That's what I thought."

Sure, reflexively anti-American critics will point out that there are mountain goats in the world with much larger horns. But longer horns likely mean a more competitive mating environment, meaning that the North American mountain goat is, when it comes to mating, confident enough in himself to keep his horns to an understated length. His are horns that say, "Sure, I got horns—here they are—but there's so much more to me than just horns coming out of my head."

The ibex (left) of Africa and Eurasia is disqualified by the bike rack, which is incredibly inconvenient to hook up to his rented Lamborghini. Likewise, Pakistan's markhor (right) has wine openers on its head and reeks of cologne.

Their first criticism rebuffed, pseudo-intellectual Europeans will likely then fall back on the old trope of scoffing at the relatively lower altitudes achieved by North American mountain goats. Yes, the reality is that North America's mountains simply leave much to be desired, with not even one in the world's top fifty peaks. But let's please not go punishing goats for the lack of compression forces in the lithospheric plates deep beneath their feet. If it were there, they would certainly climb it.

Most independent experts agree that mountain goats should be judged on two qualities: skill and looks. And the North American mountain goat more than holds its own in both departments.

First up, these animals can jump about twelve feet on their strong, thick legs. When they eventually land (on some precarious cliff in the Rocky or Cascade Mountains up to about thirteen thousand feet), it's on split cloven hooves, each with two widespread toes to increase balance. Better yet, their hooves sport a unique supergrip surface that provides additional traction. This is why you have never seen poorly shot video of a mountain goat slipping and falling into a wedding cake on *America's Funniest Home Videos*. They climb ferociously, without oxygen tanks or ropes or sherpas or gorp or pretentious lecturing about how awesome Denver is. They effortlessly navigate inclines greater than 60 degrees with ease, never once bringing up some long-ago post-climb trip to a Denver-area microbrewery. And just to show what fearless adventurers they are, females prefer to birth their young up on the highest peaks they can find. For the North American mountain goat, it's all about the thrill of the climb (and avoiding wolves). Never once is Denver mentioned.

As far as looks go, the North American mountain goat has a beard, which is because it's a mountain climber who likes having a warm face. Even the females have beards. That's how hard-core they are. They also have thick, beautiful, white coats to protect them against extreme temperatures (reaching 50 degrees below zero Fahrenheit) and against mind-numbing conversations about the importance of layering.

There is one area where the mountain goat, well, falls down. They don't have good mountain-climber names. Male mountain goats are called billies, the females are nannies, and, indicating a complete lack of imagination, they refer to their kids as kids. Those who have seen Stallone's *Cliffhanger* or read Krakauer's *Into Thin Air* know that serious climbers should really go by names like Walker, Tucker, Weathers, and Hall. Markhor and Ibex were on the right track here, but then they overshot things by adding techno music to their Web site.

Names aside, the North American mountain goat is a living tribute to all that is good and right with the continent: understated competence, a willingness to take risks, and a rich tradition of high-altitude birthing.

Well done, North American mountain goat. Here's to you.

GRADE: B+/A-

"CAN WE AT LEAST CALL HIM 'BILLIE THE KID'?"

BULLET ANT

Kingdom Animalia is rife with misleading common names. For instance, all eels are actually fish. Meanwhile, jellyfish are *not* fish, nor are they made of jelly or jam or marmalade or even preserves—sadly, "jellyfish" are mostly tentacles and painful nematocyst stingers, making the majority of the species a very poor companion to English muffins. Up on dry land, the lies persist: Badgers rarely nag or impose upon the other woodland creatures, the tarantula hawk is neither a predatory bird with eight talons nor a giant flying spider (it's a wasp), and the Great Dane is, in reality, just *pretty good* and is actually

"I'm sorry, my napkin ist gefallen. Now vat vere you sayink?"

of German extraction (the accent tends to creep back after it's had a few too many cocktails).

All of this is frustrating, complicated, and enough to make us want to start smoking again. But what to do? Well, all of us *could* make a collective decision to employ Linnaeus's clunky binomial nomenclature system in everyday conversation. And, sure, that *would* eliminate the problem of misleading animal names. But it also nearly doubles the number of names to remember. What's more, the movement would certainly lose steam the first time someone at the beach spotted a large dorsal fin tearing through the water and yelled, *"Carcharodon carcharias!"*—and then watched in erudite horror as children continued to splash around and their parents avoided eye contact with what they assumed to be a crazy Armenian tourist.

"I strongly support the use of the binomial naming system."

Then, of course, the killing would begin.

So, like it or not, we're stuck with the oft-perplexing common names.

The bullet ant (*Paraponera clavata*, lit. "anaphylactic shock and awe") of Central and South America falls into a very specific category of common names that are at first misleading ("Hmmm, it doesn't look like a bullet . . . I wonder if maybe it's fast like a bullet?"), but which then makes immediate sense when you realize you've been absent-mindedly standing on its nest this whole entire time ("Oh . . . it *hurts* like a bullet . . . okay, okay . . . I think I get it now").

The bullet ant is so named because the long, retractable syringe on its abdomen injects an incredibly painful neurotoxic peptide, poneratoxin, and it is poneratoxin that makes the bullet ant the stuff of legend among entomologists and myrmecologists.[1] Just how painful is a bullet ant's poneratoxin? Well, in simple layman's terms, it hurts like [EXPLETIVE DELETED]. More scientifically stated, it tops the Schmidt Sting Pain Index, coming in at 4.0+ on a scale of one to four, which means that the pain of a bullet-ant sting is literally off the charts, and makes one wonder if the Schmidt Sting Pain Index could use some revising.[2] In its present

---

[1] Not to mention the occasional cosmetologist who sits down on a tree stump in a Nicaraguan forest to reapply her lipstick.

[2] You first.

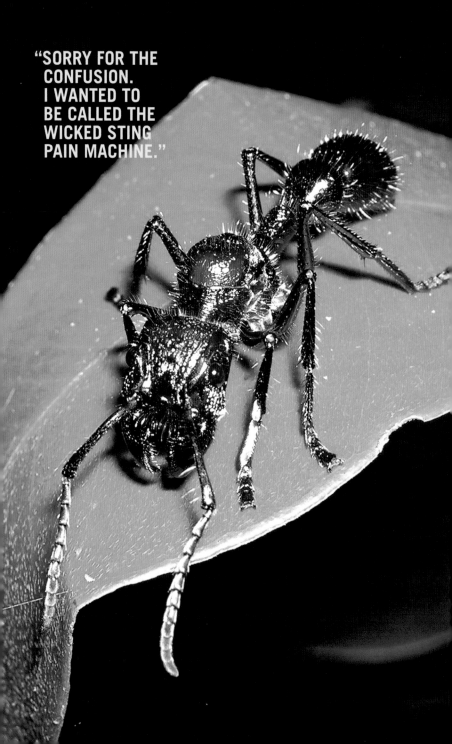

"SORRY FOR THE CONFUSION. I WANTED TO BE CALLED THE WICKED STING PAIN MACHINE."

form, the Schmidt Sting Pain Index[3] is the brainchild of Justin Schmidt, an entomologist who subjected himself to the bites and stings of horrible insects in his very favorite taxonomic order, Hymenoptera (mainly wasps, bees, and ants), in an effort to classify the pain numerically and get his picture in *Pointless Weekly*. And though it was an overnight success among entomologists, the insect pain scale never found a foothold in popular culture; as a result, the great Muhammad Ali is never described as a pugilist who could "float like a butterfly and sting like a 2.54 on the Schmidt Sting Pain Index."

Schmidt characterized the sting of a single bullet ant as "pure, intense, brilliant pain" and suggested (from self-imposed experience) that it was about thirty times more painful than the sting of a common wasp. And so the bullet ant holds the titles of both world's most hurtful insect and world's most hurtful invertebrate, while Schmidt himself remains ranked as the coolest entomologist in the cafeteria.

"Did I tell you that I let a bumblebee sting the inside of my nose? Because I did."

[3] The Schmidt Sting Pain Index is not to be confused with the Schmidt Sting Pain Scale, which Justin Schmidt developed to classify the terrible progression of Gordon Sumner's complete discography. Schmidt ranked the October 2006 release *Songs from the Labyrinth* at 3.8, describing it as "hot, smoky, searing agony. Even for $6.99."

It turns out, however, that long before Schmidt and his pain experiments, the Satere-Mawe tribesmen of Brazil had been well aware of the kind of pain available from the bullet ants. Sure, they lack the science to isolate the poneratoxin and identify its precise effect on nervous tissue, but they do have the good old common sense to collect the ants, drug them with a natural anesthetic, and weave them by the hundreds into thatched gloves for their young aspiring warriors to wear for ten minutes (a process repeated *up to twenty times* over the course of their initiation), rendering their hands burning, throbbing, useless masses of excruciating torture that lasts for hours and hours. The Satere-Mawe still perform the rite of passage to this day and seem mostly fine with it, with the exception of the few Satere-Mawe warriors who have had the eye-opening experience of attending a bar mitzvah.

"What? He gets a car? You've got to be kidding me."

Aside from having a mind-bending sting, bullet ants are huge (for an ant), with workers reaching up to one inch in length, making them the largest ant in the world. And opposite their abdominal stingers, these predatory/scavenging insects sport oversize mandibles that offer prey such as termites the choice of death by neurotoxic peptide or by a giant pair of organic pliers. Indignant termites will often ridicule this proposition as an either-or fallacy or a false dilemma, pointing out that they also have the option to escape, though they rarely complete the thought.

Given the bullet ant's small-animal/big-sting persona, Animal Review is willing to overlook its somewhat misleading common name (along with a stern admonition that it *could* be clearer: Might we suggest a simple prefix like Neurotoxic or Excruciating—or both?). The fact is, the bullet ant carries the most painful sting of any insect, so painful that simply wearing a glove filled with hundreds of bullet ants twenty times is apparently enough to make you into a warrior (though probably more than a few Satere-Mawe initiates have some unspoken concerns about how hand stinging relates to winning wars). The only real issue holding back *Paraponera clavata* is that, after all is said and done, it is still an ant. And nobody ever gets too excited about ants.[4]

GRADE: B+

 FUN FACT As a defense mechanism, some species of ants explode their own heads in a shower of toxic chemicals. Ants can be a bit dramatic sometimes.

---

[4] Except myrmecologists.

SPOTLIGHT ON: BEARS

While polls show that most people consider the species to beat in an animal-versus-animal throwdown to be a lion or tiger (with much back and forth about which of these would win) (and for the record, it's probably the lion), these questions miss the obvious fact that both would most definitely lose to a Kodiak bear as well as its smaller, aggressive cousin, the grizzly.

Consider the numbers: A male lion might weigh five hundred pounds and the largest Siberian tiger on record was over eight hundred pounds (a definite outlier; your average Joe Tiger weighs somewhere between three hundred and five hundred pounds), an adult male grizzly may weigh over one thousand pounds, and the Kodiak can top twelve hundred pounds without breaking a sweat. These bears have enormous bone and muscle density and giant claws. By contrast, the cats were designed for speed (and aloofness) and thus have comparatively low-density bones and elastic musculature. In a one-on-one fight, the bear's advantages would be unambiguous. This theory was, in fact, tested during the 1800s by bored Californians who captured grizzly bears, dug a pit, and forced the bears to square off against a variety of animals. (For the record, bulls did very poorly.) Eventually they brought in African lions, and let's just say it wasn't a banner day for them as a species and leave it at that.

Of course, the largest land carnivore is the polar bear, which has a well-earned reputation for fearlessness and ferocity. But its claws are a mere two inches or so, and it has a thinner skull and longer neck than the grizzly (adaptations for the polar bear's aquatic lifestyle). The grizzly is shorter but squatter, and polar bears have been known to be driven off by grizzlies when the snow melts and their habitats overlap. It's a bit like *West Side Story* but with less snapping and more hungry, angry bears.

Given North America's somewhat shameful animal population, it's wonderful news that all these massive, terrifying beasts huddle amongst the wilds of the continent. If you meet one in a bar, offer to buy him or her a drink. After all, they are the ones keeping the lions and tigers at bay.

ALPACA

The alpaca (*Vicugna pacos*) is a close relative of the fellow South American llama (same family, *Camelidae*, "the camel family in Latin"). The alpaca is much smaller than the llama, coming in at about 125 pounds and around four feet tall at adulthood, whereas a llama may weigh as much as forty thousand pounds and be well over seven hundred feet tall.

Depending on your place of residence, perhaps you've seen ads late at night that extol the glories of alpaca farming. According to these ads, the "alpaca lifestyle" is an easy and extremely profitable one that beats the alpaca-fiber pants off the suckers who actually work for a living. However, like most investment opportunities involving hoofed South American animals, raising alpacas may not be the cash machine that creepy on-camera testimonials claim it is. A quick Internet search of the term *alpaca scam* reveals all manner of aspersion cast upon the American alpaca industrial complex, from the obvious (there's really not much of a market for alpaca wool in the U.S.) to the conspiratorial (that it's all a massive pyramid scheme that eventually has to collapse).

Animal Review does not take an official position on the "alpaca lifestyle" and holds no positions in any alpaca stocks. People are encouraged to do their own research and form their own conclusions before deciding whether or not to buy alpacas.

Native to South America (where they're well suited to the frigid, high-altitude lifestyle in the Andes Mountains), alpacas have been used as beasts of burden, for meat, and, most notably, for their fine fiber, which is considered much finer than llama fiber by people who pay attention to this kind of thing.

Phenotypically, an alpaca looks like a weird sheep/horse/goat mix, and indeed many leading authors of books that grade animals believe that this is precisely what it is, originating somewhere in North America during the Pleistocene era. Perhaps, following a

"MIGHT NOT
BE FOR YOU
. . . IF YOU
LIKE WORKING
FOR A LIVING.
LOSER."

horrifying series of mating errors between sheep, a horse, and some goats, the newly minted alpaca traveled to South America, and, quite honestly, the sheep, horses, and goats were happy to see their secret shame leave. The alpaca found a new home down south, where it was immediately beloved for its agreeably stupid disposition, which, by the way, only reinforces the idea that it is the product of interspecies breeding that should never have occurred.

Weirded out yet?

Alpacas hit their stride in the Incan Empire, where wealth was in part demonstrated by the number of alpacas one owned. And here's where the dumb alpaca has a lot to answer for. Only fourteen large animals have ever been successfully domesticated: sheep, goats, cows, pigs, horses, Arabian camels, Bactrian camels, llamas and alpacas, donkeys, reindeer, water buffalos, yaks, Bali cattle, and mithans (a type of ox). Of these, llamas and alpacas are the only New World domesticates.[1]

So flash forward to 1532, when Spanish Conquistador Francisco Pizarro and 168 of his men show up with horses in what is now Peru. And in about one day, the Spanish and their horses defeated thousands of Incan fighters in open battle, captured the Incan god-king Atahualpa, and generally made Spain look pretty awesome.

This stunning victory was largely thanks to the Spanish caballeros, who rode into battle astride massive steeds that were perfect for terrorizing Incans who had never seen a horse, let alone many angry

---

[1] This does not include dogs, which is probably good, since let's not lump in dogs with alpacas.

ones. So frightening were the warhorses that even the Conquistadors themselves were scared of what they had gotten themselves into. Recalled one of Pizarro's men: "We really whipped them into a frenzy, and quite honestly, I was worried Old Kicky would freak out. But he ended up being pretty cool about it."[2]

And while the Spanish horses were busy conquering an empire, the Incans' alpacas were standing around looking for some more grass to eat.

Thanks.

Between the generally creepy appearance, suspect breeding, alleged pyramid schemes, and allowing an ancient empire to be defeated in an afternoon, alpacas have a lot to answer for. We wish them well in their future endeavors.

GRADE: F

[2] *I Come in Peace . . . Wait, No I Don't: Memoirs of a Conquistador*, by Roberto La Paz Martinez.

KOALA

Pretty much every animal in Australia is terrifying. Between the spiders, sharks, crocodiles, box jellyfish, drunk pleasure boaters, Russell Crowe, and six of the ten deadliest snakes in the world, you're not really safe anywhere on the continent. Yet the travel brochures are conspicuously silent on this matter. Sure, they offer up glossy photos of the Sydney Opera House and go on and on about modern expressionist design. But it's what they don't show you—the hordes of lethal creatures teeming in the shadows (and everywhere else)—that makes the grueling fourteen-hour flight[1] seem, in retrospect, like a really bad idea.

Tonight:
—Pain, sweating, vomiting, and seizures
—Also, Opera Australia presents Mozart's *The Magic Flute*

---

[1] After watching a terrible movie (probably *Australia*), eating, *and* sleeping, there's still seven hours to go. It really is the worst. Then there's the jet lag. And that's all before you get bitten by a brown snake. So to answer your question, just go to Jamaica for your honeymoon.

Even Australia's "cute and cuddly" animals are more than happy to open a gaping wound on your face. The koala bear (*Phascolarctos cinereus*, lit. "come a little closer so I can permanently disfigure you") is a perfect example. Nevertheless, upon spotting a koala, most tourists feel compelled to cancel their hotel reservations and spend the remainder of their vacation spooning with this plush marsupial in the nook of a eucalyptus tree.[2] It's difficult to express how much of a mistake this is.

"Oooh, look, it's an adorable little . . . AAAAHHHH!! GET IT OFF ME!!"

Unlike most of Australia's fauna, koalas really have no reason to be so uncool to tourists. While the overwhelming majority of predators Down Under are naturally driven to extreme violence by the very nature of their existence, the koala's lifestyle is a study in easy.

First of all, koalas sleep a good eighteen to twenty-two hours a day and still have the temerity to call themselves nocturnal. They eat only one thing—poisonous, low-calorie, disgusting eucalyptus leaves—so it's not like the other animals are falling all over themselves to compete for it. And since eucalyptus leaves are 50 percent water, providing all the moisture a koala needs, they don't even have to get out of bed for a drink. In fact, the name *koala* is derived from the aborigine word meaning "no drink." Apparently they don't have a word for "irrationally angry fuzzy pseudo-bear."

---

[2] That's exactly how the famous children's toy tycoon Frederick August Otto (F.A.O.) Schwarz died during an ill-fated stuffed animal research expedition in 1911. According to legend, his final words were "Gentlemen . . . do . . . not . . . spoon . . . with . . . that . . . thing."

"Pwease, pwease. Don't let the big bad bulldozerers hurted me, Sheila. It's okay if I call you Sheila, right?"

So koalas have it good by any standard of good, except for the fact that Australians are steadily destroying their habitats. But being cranky doesn't help their cause—and therein lies the problem with koalas: They just don't put their superior cuteness to work for them. If they were smart, koalas would be jumping from the eucalyptus trees right into the arms of tourists, showering them with kisses, and whispering gentle reminders that they are actually marsupials and are in no way related to bears who *are* quite mean, and if we could just stop calling them bears, well, then that would be super-duper. Naturally, this speech would be peppered with high-pitched giggling.

Next they would show off their trademark marsupial pouches, briefly discuss their anatomical differences from placental mammals (giggle, giggle), and then take our hands and lead us on a quick tour of the magical eucalyptus forest ("C'mon everybody!"). They'd explain how humans are encroaching on their territories, forcing them onto the ground and putting them at risk to dogs and cars, which claim more than four thousand koala lives each year. (At this point the giggling would noticeably taper off.)

The koalas would then produce a crudely drawn graph depicting declining koala life expectancy, complete with spelling errors and backwards letters that we'd find absolutely endearing. And while we were looking at the charts, the koalas would surreptitiously rub some eucalyptus in their eyes to get those tear ducts going, and that would be that. Who can resist a crying teddy bear? Nobody, *that's* who. We'd be stalwart defenders of the koala cause forever. We'd go to *war* with Australia to save them. Our president would be standing atop a pile of eucalyptus rubble with a megaphone saying, "I can hear you, I can hear you. The rest of the world hears you. And the people who knocked these trees down will hear all of us soon."

It's called using your cuteness.

But, sadly, koalas haven't figured this out yet. Instead, if you try to hug a wild koala, or get involved personally in any way, you get a razor-sharp claw across the face. If you still feel the need to hug a koala, and you're not a huge fan of deep lacerations, you'd be much better off buying one of those little clippy ones for your shirt collar and calling it a day.

GRADE: C-

FUN FACT A group of kangaroos is called a mob. And odds are, it's an angry one.

SPOTLIGHT ON: APES

Family Hominidae (aka the Great Apes, aka the Brain Trust) consists of humans, gorillas, common chimpanzees, orangutans, and bonobos. These are our closest evolutionary relatives, and all apes are incredibly intelligent, all use tools, and everyone probably has a favorite among them, though probably almost nobody's is the bonobo. And all are violent—like hugely violent—*except* for the bonobos.

The bonobo and the chimpanzee share the same genus (*Pan*), look much alike, and are separated geographically by the Congo River. But bonobos are different for their lack of antisocial behavior. Chimps organize war parties against other chimps and will commit murder; male gorillas commit infanticide; orangutans commit identity theft and star in Clint Eastwood movies.

But not bonobos—they are decidedly peaceful creatures who play well with others.[1] And here's what's important: They are the only apes whose social arrangements are, if not matriarchal, then decidedly female-centered. Take from that what you will.

But before reading too much into this, it's important to note that bonobos are also really into free love, mating casually and copiously with numerous partners to settle disputes, show affection, and pass the time. So we have male-centered ape societies that are given to violence, and then a lone female-centered species that is fairly relaxed in its morals but manages to keep everything calm and relatively harmonious. Are we saying that women are a more peaceful gender? Well, this isn't exactly a scientific study, but hey, that's never stopped anyone from drawing conclusions about the benefits of weird teas. So why not bring it up at the next cocktail party?

---

[1] Though like chimps, bonobos have been observed hunting monkeys for food. But, you know, you gotta eat.

"WHAT
WOULD
YOUR
MOTHER
SAY?"

SKUNK

It may look pretty in your pictures, but Nature is one massive evolutionary battleground. So striking are the similarities between evolution's battles and those fought with tanks and planes that biologists actually use the term "arms race" to describe the defense and counterdefense strategies that microbes, parasites, plants, and animals continually develop to do combat with ever-increasing efficiency. It's war out there, plain and simple. Were it not for the enormous time scales required for evolutionary battles to play out, journalists would be embedded right now with the various divisions of Kingdom Animalia.

"All we know right now, Suzanne, is that some lizards are surviving long enough to reproduce."

A typical example of an evolutionary arms race can be seen in the Great War between Kingdom Plantae and Kingdom Animalia. It went down something like this: Plants arise. Animals arise and eat plants. Plants grow thorns. Animals counter with thick skin and fur. Plants say, "Yeah? Get a load of these toxins. We hope you like diarrhea." Animals declare diarrhea a gratuitous "prelude to war" and introduce simple digestive enzymes to break down the toxins. Plants make vague conciliatory gestures at mediated peace talks while their military secretly draws up plans for deadlier toxins. Animals appeal to the defense sector to begin work on a liver. Propped up by surging nationalism and xenophobia at home, plants begin testing bark. *Et cetera*.

The oleander delegates confer as negotiations break down in Geneva.

Of course, deadly arms races between animals have likewise been raging ever since there were animals. For example, the crab would not have engineered its infamous Claw O' Hurt had the sea snail not first wrapped itself in a thick shell. And so forth. The list is endless and depressing, but let's cut to the chase: Animal Review is pleased to announce a winner in the evolutionary arms race.

The skunk.

The skunk (family Mephitidae) vaulted itself out of the contest some time ago with a stunning technical achievement that rocked Kingdom Animalia to its very core and made most of Nature's weapons irrelevant overnight. The skunk was the first animal to enter the nuclear age.

"Get me Harry Truman on the horn."

As with man's first fission bomb, the skunk's weapon represented a quantum leap in technology, although the techniques varied slightly. Instead of imploding a subcritical sphere of plutonium to maximize the plutonium's density and trigger a chain reaction, the skunk went with a horrendous yellow oil composed of sulfurous thiol compounds and a simple delivery system of two scent glands[1] positioned on either side of the anus. Gross? Certainly. But the anus had its advantages during top-secret testing phases, because who's going to look there?

In a host of ways, the skunk is the Israel of animaldom. Both Israel and skunks are surrounded by hostile neighbors, but in both cases their would-be aggressors know full well that attacking would only mean their own demise, or at least a long bath in tomato juice followed by days of solitude. The central difference between Israel and skunks is the fact that Israel has never admitted to owning any nukes, whereas skunks paint themselves black and give themselves

---

[1] With a nod to the Manhattan Project, the skunk calls the scent glands Fat Man and Little Boy.

white racing stripes as a way of advertising that, yes, they are skunks, and yes, they're ready to mess you up bad.

Possession of the bomb has other bonuses. If you've ever seen a skunk, they tend to walk around freely, even in large open fields, without so much as a hint of fear of foxes, wolves, or other predators.[2] Just like Israel, they feel no need to seek cover under logs or constantly whip their heads about like those manic, poorly armed squirrels. Many skunks are overweight, because they do nothing but eat insects, worms, frogs, and berries all day without ever running away from anything. And they have lousy vision that they've never had to bother evolving because, hey, as long as you can see the big red button, that's all you really need to see.

After leapfrogging the other animals with high tech, the skunk moved into a sort of Cold War with what used to be its natural predators. Instead of tearing each other apart in open skirmishes with crude claws and teeth, skunks and wolves are now relegated to giving carefully crafted statements and then putting on large headsets to wait for their opponents' response to be translated.

Even in such civilized surroundings, the wolf still looks nervous. Here's to military technology and brains over brawn.

GRADE: A

 **FUN FACT** Gorillas live in family groups of anywhere from two to thirty gorillas, all in a modest suburban five-bedroom home outside Saint Paul.

---

[2] A notable exception is the great horned owl, which has no sense of smell. But you'd think that after a while the owl would get tired of eating alone.

SKY

BALD EAGLE

The bald eagle (*Haliaeetus leucocephalus*, lit. "No pictures, please") is the entitled blue blood of Kingdom Animalia. The national bird of the United States and longtime spokesmodel for the endangered species list,[1] the bald eagle just *looks* like animal royalty. With its terrifyingly sharp beak, long talons, stark yellow eyes against a bright white head, and a wingspan that can reach eight feet, the bald eagle has style to spare (and is a sight to behold in a tailored suit), making it a natural celebrity whose sense of self-importance is hard to overestimate.

"This had better be organic."

---

[1] Though it became a victim of its own success when in 1995 it was moved to the threatened species category and then removed from the threatened list altogether in 1999. But shooting a bald eagle is still punishable by prison time, so Winchester's new 12-gauge Super Eagle Loads (4) probably aren't the wisest use of your money at this time.

"Wait, the one with the eagle on its money? Hey—you first."

The bald eagle got its start when it was cast as America's national bird by the Continental Congress and formally emblazoned on the Great Seal of the United States in 1782.[2] The selection made plenty of sense, too. For starters, it gives the immediate impression of a bird not to be trifled with, which is what you want when foreign countries are deciding whether or not to attack you (a decision usually based on what's on the back of your country's quarters).[3]

The bald eagle does in fact back up its terrifying visage with its deeds: cruising thermal convection currents at ten thousand feet, it can look out over a three-square-mile area with its excellent eyesight and then swoop down to grab prey at one hundred miles per hour,

---

[2] This prompted Ben Franklin to complain in a letter to his daughter that the bald eagle was a poor choice as a national bird. True story—he realized it had "bad moral character" long before anyone else. Franklin's suggestion was to use the wild turkey, because it was "a little vain & silly [but] a Bird of Courage." But one can only imagine how depressing Thanksgiving dinner would be if we were all dining on our national symbol. Plus there would be two drumsticks on the presidential seal, which would almost certainly make the bully pulpit a lot less intimidating.

[3] By way of contrast, Kenya's national bird is the rooster, a selection that was unquestionably the work of a committee. Probably a committee in a university. Speaking of which, the rooster is also the national symbol of France. If anyone loves committees, it's the French.

making the rabbit's daily commute a bit of a living nightmare. What's more, the bald eagle brought range—literally—appearing in all of the contiguous United States, offering an ecumenicalism that assured nobody would feel left out (except for, eventually, Hawaii, whose state bird is the nene—aka the Hawaiian Goose—which was chosen in an effort to let everyone know that they had absolutely nothing to fear from Hawaii).

"Sparrow, robin, duck . . . wait, what's this magnificent creature with stunning two-tone plumage and a super-intimidating beak? How about that one?"

Soon enough, the bald eagle was ensconced in the national mythology and immediately started booking gigs appearing on money, collectible plates, inspirational posters, Boy Scout badges, and biker tattoos. Naturally, the fawning worship of an entire nuclear-armed nation went to its head, and soon not even its massive nests (the largest of any bird in North America) could hold its swelling ego. Unfortunately, at some point the bald eagle convinced itself that it had actually *earned* everything that had been handed to it on a silver platter emblazoned with its own image.

"I work really hard. Now if you'll excuse me, I'm off to get tapped for Skull and Bones and then pose for an Abercrombie catalog."

The bald eagle would have been content to spend its time majestically soaring high above Earth, looking down its razor-sharp nose at everything below, were it not for its sudden and rapid decline in the mid-twentieth century. This was attributed to hunting and various pollutants (most famously the insecticide DDT, which, while not deadly to adult birds, interfered with their calcium metabolism and left them either sterile or able to lay only extremely thin-shelled eggs). In 1967, the bald eagle was listed as an endangered species, and shortly thereafter DDT was banned. Over the subsequent decades, the bald eagle population made a significant recovery, but whereas another bird might have taken this brush with near-extinction as a wake-up call about what the heck it's doing with its life, the scarcity implied by membership on the endangered species list only reinforced

"Oh, you've never tried getting on the endangered species list? You simply *must*."

the bald eagle's self-conception as an *avis raris* to whom normal rules of behavior do not apply.

As its numbers have recovered, the bald eagle's ego recovered doubly, and it is now convinced that it can do anything. It is indeed fortunate that bald eagles can fly, because even if they couldn't, there would be a high likelihood that one night, after a lot of Maker's Mark, they would most surely feel the need to show everyone at the party they could.

GRADE: C+

→ **FUN FACT** Migrating birds can take semiconscious naps in flight. Which is why it's important to pass federal legislation outlawing this kind of thing. Birds with cell phones are fine, though, so long as they use a hands-free device. But no texting please.

LOCUST

If you're a farmer (or someone who depends on a farmer) in certain arid or semiarid desert regions of Africa, Asia, and India, or if you're the parent of a middle-school girl, you're all too familiar with the horrors we are about to describe. Locusts are, without a doubt, the most destructive insect force in the world. Fear precedes them. Death, chaos, and untold human misery lie in their wake. The locust is Nature's teenage girl.

Teen girls and locusts really do have a lot in common. The most obvious connection is that both are biblical plagues. Locusts appeared in the devastating eighth plague of Egypt, described in Exodus 10:1–20. Teenage girls were the eleventh and final bonus plague, summoned by Moses after the will of the Egyptian Pharaoh had already been broken by the tenth plague, Death of Firstborn. As the story goes, the teenage girls were so great in number that they blocked out the sun.

The desert locust (*Shistocerca gregaria,* lit. "Mom, you're embarrassing me") is the quintessential locust. It is one of a dozen or so spe-

"MY PARENTS SAY I CAN'T HAVE AN iPHONE. I WISH I WAS NEVER BORN."

cies of "grasshoppers" whose appearance and temperament actually *transform* as their social conditions change. This will sound familiar to any parents out there. Locusts go through distinct physical and psychological phases before they set out to destroy the world.

Normally, juvenile desert locusts are solitary, shy, nonswarming creatures. Entomologists call this the "solitarious phase." During their solitarious phase, locusts are green in color and tend to avoid others. They walk down the hallway toward their locker, clutching their books to their chest, avoiding eye contact and trying to position their hair in a way that best conceals their acne. They are polite, reserved, and pleasantly self-conscious as they silently eat vegetation. They send thank-you cards to their grandmother without being reminded. Parenting is a breeze.

It's only when they start to make friends that desert locusts and teen girls become horrible. If their food source gets scarce, locusts will move closer and closer together to compete for the same resource. At some critical point, the crowding triggers a metamorphosis and the locusts enter the feared "gregarious phase." This is characterized by a remarkable shift in appearance and attitude and a precipitous drop in grade-point average. Their color changes from a friendly green to a more sinister multicolored yellowish black. They start smoking and they now keep eyeliner, to apply as soon as they leave the house, in their Juicy Couture purse. And, of course, they begin to cluster and swarm—sacrificing self for the ever-shifting whim of the group. Locusts in the gregarious phase are no longer individuals. They are monstrous cliques.

Swarming, gregarious locusts are terrible to both themselves and everyone around them. The pressure to follow is fierce and often contradictory. Locusts are normally vegetarians, but if a locust becomes injured (usually when bitten by a locust who accuses it of talking to its boyfriend) or if it shows any indication of weakness (such as listening to the Jonas Brothers or wearing off-brand jeans), the locusts nearby will take it as a sign to pounce on the poor thing and cannibalize it on the spot. Swarm life, like ninth grade, can be a difficult time.

"Yeah, Heather, you're such a loser who reads and understands and stuff. We're totally going to cannibalize you after school."

Locust swarms are capable of destruction that qualifies as a natural disaster. One swarm can cover 460 square miles and contain billions of locusts. And that's *before* Miley Cyrus takes the stage. A single locust can eat its own weight in plants in a day, which means that a swarm can devour about 423 million pounds of life-giving crops and green vegetation in twenty-four hours. All they want to do is eat, but God help the locust that goes from a size three to a size eight over the summer. That's social suicide. At that point, it might as well enroll in a school for locusts with special needs.

And locusts are not just an ancient problem—they are still a great threat today. In 2004, a plague swept through swaths of Africa in dark ominous clouds that were miles in length. In the end, the Islamic Republic of Mauritania estimated that nearly 50 percent of its cereal-production capability had been destroyed. Meanwhile, neighboring countries such as Mali and Senegal reported unprecedented spikes in MySpace traffic that brought their telecom infrastructure to its knees. Shortly after the problem was fixed, the systems crashed again and actually caught on fire as the locusts furiously took online

1. Female locust lays eggs in soil, then files for divorce.

Egg

Life Cycle of the Desert Locust

2. Shy, green-colored, "solitary" locust emerges. Goes as morally lax mermaid on Halloween.

3. Solitary locusts hang out, turn dark-ish color, get butterfly tattoos on lower back.

4. New "gregarious" locusts swarm, binge, say things like "that's sick," have low-level freak-outs on people they don't really know at otherwise nice parties, ruin whole countries.

quizzes that asked things like "What kind of ice cream are you?" and "Are you the perfect girlfriend?" It was an unmitigated nightmare.

In such extreme cases, there aren't many options for the afflicted, especially if the plague strikes a poor, third-world country. One can hope that a well-funded, multinational pesticide campaign can curb the spread of the swarm. Or one can just try to wait it out until a locust matures a little, finds a nice boyfriend, and, with any luck, turns green again and eventually gets accepted to an out-of-state community college.

GRADE: F

OWL

Ever since man has been able to stand on two legs and communicate complex thoughts, he's been running around saying things that just aren't true. Crude cave drawings indicate that much of our primitive gossip was directed at stick figures, who seem to have gone extinct at some point (probably to get away from all the gossip). We then turned our vitriolic whisper machine on animals. The evidence from carbon dating is crystal clear: Man has been assigning random, petty, conflicting, and downright stupid meanings to animals for thousands of years, and the owl (order Strigiformes, lit. "What did *I* do?") has been on the receiving end of much of it. Thus have the fascinating adaptations of these mostly nocturnal raptors been lost in the deep sea of human ignorance.

Even before we were very good at writing stuff, we were impugning the owl's character. In the Egyptian hieroglyphic system, a draw-

"I fly silently because special feathers on my wings reduce air turbulence. Which is why when you dream about an owl you're going to die. Isn't that right, the Apache people of North America?"

ing of an owl represented the letter *M*. Now, one might imagine that this would be something of an honor, being a letter in some powerful nation's alphabet. But to the Egyptians, owls symbolized death, and so the owl was sometimes drawn with a broken leg to keep it from springing to life and murdering people. Which begs the question: Why even have letters that can kill you if you accidentally forget to maim them ahead of time?

It's not just the Egyptians—nearly every major human civilization in history has opined on owls. The Greeks thought it was Athena's bird (a sagacious protector), and if you had a drachma for every Greek warrior who cheered in delight upon seeing an owl before battle, you'd live like a king (a democratically elected one). By contrast, the Romans were more glass-half-empty owl speculators, believing the presence of an owl to be a sure sign of defeat. Which makes you wonder how history might have been different if Julius Caesar had seen an owl on the way to the Senate to meet his old pal Brutus for lunch.

The list goes on. African tribes often saw the owl as pure evil. Australian aborigines will tell you that the call of an owl precedes the death of a loved one. Transylvanian farmers were known to try to

"My face is shaped like a satellite dish in order to collect and amplify sound, and I can alter its shape with small muscles in my face. Of course, I could also be a witch."

scare off owls by walking around naked. And in the good ol' U.S. of A we draw owls in cap and gown, put some glasses on them, and cart them out to sell literacy programs. Or at least figure out how many licks it takes to get through a lollipop.

"I have excellent stereoscopic vision and my eyes maximize available light. Oh, look, there's a naked Transylvanian farmer. Terrific. Good thing I also have three eyelids, which I'm now going to shut."

Perhaps it's best to stick to what the owl *can't* do. None of the roughly 220 species of owls can help you communicate with the dead. Nailing them to barn doors will not prevent lightning. They won't protect livestock from evil spirits, they don't bring bad luck or bad weather, and they most certainly do not devour newborn babies. We won't name names here, nations of the world, but you know who you are.

Enough. While it may be more thrilling to assign owls supernatural ability, it is time to accept the owl for what it is: a nearly perfect bird of prey, a stunningly well-engineered flying machine, and probably a clairvoyant of the devil.

GRADE: B+

SPOTLIGHT ON: BIRDING

THE ANIMAL REVIEW NAMING GUIDE FOR RELUCTANT BIRDERS

The hobby of birding is extremely embarrassing and also very time-consuming. Birding usually occurs in places like the Salton Sea, just outside of Palm Springs, in 90-plus-degree heat (after a four-hour drive, on a Sunday, when you could just as easily have spent the time checking e-mail between naps but instead your beloved sister is insisting that you'll really like birding if you just give it a chance). Still, people do it. And worse, they sometimes insist on bringing their friends and family along. There's little we can do to prevent this, but if you ever get guilted into a birding trip, here are easy instructions for fitting in, or at least being so annoying that you don't get invited back.

Good luck out there.

INSTRUCTIONS FOR NAMING BIRDS:
- Observe bird (or not)
- Make one selection from each of the four groups
- Add your selections to one of the example birding sentences provided, or invent your own

Congratulations, you're an ornithologist.

THE ANIMAL REVIEW NAMING GUIDE FOR RELUCTANT BIRDERS

GROUP 1	GROUP 2	GROUP 3	GROUP 4
Northern	Brown	Speckled	Warbler
Southern	Red	Spotted	Warbler of Paradise
Eastern	Blue	Throated	Gorbler
Western	Green	Tufted	King Gorbler
Canadian	Yellow	Bellied	Schmorbler
European	Burnt Sienna	Billed	Jack Schmorbler
Mexican	Purple	Legged	Mumbler
Moroccan		Whiskered	Squacker
Cleveland		Headed	Loon
		Tailed	Starling
		Crowned	Agent Starling
		Rumped	Lark
		Shouldered	Gull
		Ringed	Sandgrouse
		Toed	Egret
		Eared	Plover
		Winged	Pterodactyl
		Backed	Finch

EXAMPLE BIRDING SENTENCES

"If I'm not mistaken, that's a (group 1) (group 2) (group 3) (group 4). Awesome. Let's break for lunch."

"Ooohhh, that's a (group 1) (group 2) (group 3) (group 4). Very rare. Look at the plumage. Isn't it just grand? Also, it's getting kind of late, don't you think?"

"I believe we're in the presence of a (group 1) (group 2) (group 3) (group 4). Can we go now?"

"I think I caught a glimpse of a lovely (group 1) (group 2) (group 3) (group 4), but it's gone now. Hey, did we bring enough water? Maybe we should get going. I'm thinking about your safety here, Karen."

VULTURE

One thing is for sure: Vultures are nothing if not characters. What other bird, lacking many predators anyway, still maintains a defensive mechanism that consists of vomiting up rotten meat? What other animal is so resistant to the bacterial disease botulism that it can ingest enough botulinus to kill three hundred thousand guinea pigs and not even break into a cold sweat? And what other creature lacks sweat glands *anyway* and instead excretes uric acid to cool off *and* to kill bacteria that might be left on its legs from a dead gazelle? No other animal does all of these things. Which, among other reasons, is why a vulture would be hands down the weirdest roommate you could ever have.[1]

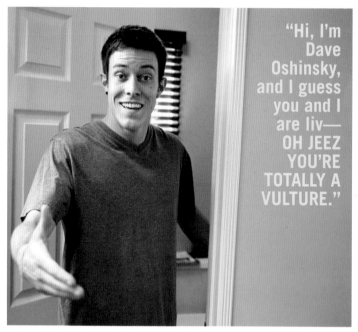

"Hi, I'm Dave Oshinsky, and I guess you and I are liv— OH JEEZ YOU'RE TOTALLY A VULTURE."

---

[1] With the possible exception of a music major. Good luck there.

All vultures are large, carrion-eating birds (i.e., they fly around looking for dead things to eat)[2] with bald heads (to keep too much bacteria and viscera from getting in their feathers during gastrointestinal dives into a dead bison). For many years, it was thought that all vultures were raptors in order Falconiformes (lit. "falcon I form es"). Well, you can imagine the bird egg on many an ornithologist's face when it was discovered in 1994 that the New World vultures of North America share a common ancestor with storks and ibises. *Whoa.* Though both are members of order Accipitriformes within class Aves, it turns out that New World vultures are actually members of family Cathartidae (which includes seven species of vulture) while the Old World vultures of Africa, Asia, and Europe are members of family Accipitridae (fifteen species). So nice work, DNA analysts. Now get back to solving crimes in Las Vegas on TV like you're supposed to.

This fact that both Old World vultures and New World vultures decided to go bald and dig around in dead things is an example of convergent evolution, where unrelated lineages acquire the same traits when, for example, it becomes clear that there is just a *ton* of dead stuff lying around for the taking. While both Old World and New World vultures suffer from congenital alopecia, there are differences, and these distinctions are important considerations when deciding if you want to room together for another year. First of all, Old World vultures have relatively strong feet, with clasping talons that allow them to carry dead animal parts and/or make a quick pizza run, while New World vultures have relatively weak, chickenesque feet more suited to running across the street to claim a rare on-campus parking spot while you find a place to turn the car around. Unfortunately, these vultures cannot carry pizzas with their feet, though they also can't bring rotten animal flesh back to the room either. The beaks of the New World vultures are relatively weaker than the beaks of

---

[2] The exception is the palm nut vulture, *Gyphohierax angolensis*, which feeds principally on the fruit of the oil palm. This is the vulture everyone crosses their fingers for when they open the envelope with their rooming assignment and they see the name "A. Vulture."

their Old World counterparts, which might be important if you need them to open jars. Finally, some New World vultures have the ability to smell (which they use to help locate food), whereas Old World vultures lack a sense of smell (a small disadvantage in the search for decomposing flesh, but a *huge* advantage after a rotting dead animal is found and they have to stick their heads into it). As for your rooming situation, the sense of smell might come in handy if there's a fire in the dorm. Then again, no sense of smell could be nice, too, given the hygiene habits of your typical college freshman.

Vultures have a long history in human mythology and ritual. In ancient Egypt, the vulture was the representative of Nekhbet, the mother goddess who protected Upper Egypt. In other parts of Africa, vultures were synonymous with love, and their ability to show up wherever something died inspired a belief that vultures dream the location of food or use some kind of telepathy.[3] In the Parsi branch of Zoroastrianism, the dead are placed upon so-called Towers of Silence, where the elements and vultures hasten decomposition.[4] And in modern times, vultures are seen as symbols of the legal profession, because, as with lawyers, nobody likes vultures until they need one (whether to check a contract or clean up a rotting elephant carcass).

While the work of the vulture is seemingly unpleasant to outsiders, it is nevertheless important. By cleaning up the animal carcasses littering the plains and valleys of the world, vultures keep the environment clean, preventing the spread of

---

[3] Whatever it is, it sure ain't smell. Okay, fine, it's amazing eyesight.

[4] The term "Tower of Silence" is actually attributed to a translator for the British in India named Robert Murphy. Parsi communities in India still actively use Towers of Silence, most of which are located in Mumbai. Incidentally, the name *Parsi* should give you a hint as to where they come from, i.e., Iran (Parsi < Pars < Persia[n]). For whatever it's worth, there is an amazing book on the Zoroastrian practices at UCLA called *A Zoroastrian Tapestry: Art, Religion & Culture* (Pheroza J. Godrej and Firoza Punthakey Mistree, eds.). They don't grade Towers of Silence, but it's still worthwhile.

"I DON'T KNOW WHAT HER PROBLEM IS, BUT YOUR FEET SMELL JUST FINE TO ME, BRO."

"$380/hour x 42 billable hours = $15,960. Guess who's going prelaw? Raw-wwwwhhhk, dude!"

diseases like rabies and anthrax. A kettle of circling vultures is a sign of a healthy ecosystem. Contrary to popular belief, vultures do not circle dying animals; they are probably playing, preparing for a long flight by coasting on thermal updrafts, or just trying to weird out a rival fraternity. And by the way, when the vultures *do* find food and land to dig out its innards, they no longer form a *kettle* but instead a *venue* of vultures. Those kind of odd and surprising parts of their personality are why you should probably live with a vulture for all four years of college.

GRADE: A-

➤ **FUN FACT** The arctic tern has, by far, the most horrendous migration of any bird. A round trip can total up to thirty thousand miles, and there's always a screaming baby.

PIGEON

Like *shark*, *snake*, and *skunk*, the word *pigeon* holds a multitude of meanings, not all of which refer to animals.[1] *Pigeon* can mean the feral pigeons (*Columba livia*, lit. "Got bird poop?") seen strutting, cooing, and looking for handouts in cities worldwide. It can be used to indicate the domestic pigeon (*Columba livia domestica*, lit. "Got bird poop domestically?") that has given rise to numerous remarkable varieties and is descended from the rock pigeon (also *Columba livia*, also "Got bird poop?"), found living in cliffs of Europe, North Africa, and western Asia. In slang, *pigeon* can be a noun meaning "one who is easily swindled, a dupe," or "an attractive girl"; as a verb it can mean "to cheat" (e.g., "I got pigeoned, and consequently I paid a lot for this muffler"). "Pigeon English" is also the name of a simple dialect used between foreign merchants in China, though the

"Even I get confused. And when I get confused, I poop on statues."

---

[1] Some examples of animal names that *don't* contain multitudinous meanings include *bumblebee bat*, *kakapo*, *solenodon*, and *sea otter*.

general term for such a language, *pidgin*, may or may not be derived from *pigeon*.[2]

Most people's experience is limited to the feral pigeons, which are mostly descended from escaped (or misplaced) domestic pigeons.[3] Wild pigeons were first domesticated by human beings thousands of years ago as part of Pharaoh Hotepsekhemwy's plan to ruin the local statues. All three groups interbreed happily. Feral pigeons are Nature's panhandlers, spending their days covering sidewalks and park benches in nitrogenous waste[4] while scrounging around for seeds, popcorn, chunks of leftover pita, discarded bagels, muffin crumbs, and parts of breakfast burritos. Some people fear that they carry disease, and though pigeon droppings can transmit the fungal diseases cryptococcosis and histoplasmosis, risk to humans is small, and, contrary to popular worry, feral pigeons do not spread bird flu (though they're working on it). Other people consider them part of the ambience of city life, and still others find their shamelessness and complete lack of self-respect a source of cheap entertainment.

The fecundity of urban pigeons is, however, not open for interpretation. Cityscapes are not altogether different from the cliffs that rock pigeons use to nest (although cliffs don't have the Outback Steakhouse), so pigeons find them a fine place for making more pigeons. And this is what they do with whatever time remains after

---

[2] "Pigeon English" may be named for the pigeon because it was used to send short messages between people who were separated (linguistically). Pidgins are not the native language of any speech community but are found worldwide. They are first and foremost utilitarian, marked by an uncomplicated clausal structure, reduction of syllable codas and consonant clusters, and a lack of tones and morphophonemic variation. Oh, and the use of reduplication to represent plurals and superlatives (duh).

[3] All American feral pigeons are descended from domestic pigeons, which were introduced by Jamestown settlers. Because when you're looking to colonize the New World, don't forget the pigeons.

[4] Birds lack urinary bladders and excrete unwarranted nitrogen from degraded proteins and amino acids as uric acid in droppings, and though this adaptation saves water, when it's your job to clean the Civil War cannon in the town square, Evolution's judgment probably seems fairly shortsighted.

"Sure, we could go check out art at the Met . . . or we could go throw bread at the twenty-sixth president and watch pigeons fight. Who's in?"

looking for handouts, squeegeeing the windows of unwilling motorists, and hitting up passersby for donations to a suspicious music camp for disadvantaged pigeon children that they can never quite explain with their tattered clipboard and wrinkled brochure.

Pigeons will nest almost anywhere—ledges, vents, air-conditioning units, drainage pipes, awnings, your bike seat—wherever. Beyond the nests themselves, pigeon waste is acidic and, along with the fungi it contains, is corrosive to metal and concrete.[5] Since recent studies indicate that most cities are made from concrete and metal, this can be problematic if a city's design calls for concrete and metal structures remaining intact. (And, at a basic level, getting bird poop on your hair/jacket/bike seat is almost nobody's ideal way to start the day.) One effective method of population control has been the reintroduction of peregrine falcons, which feed on pigeons, which

---

[5] Rumor is that some pigeons will use this as a way to break through your bike lock.

Government in action.

has also aided the recovery of the once-endangered peregrine. Still other cities have attempted to deal with nesting and overpopulation issues by providing specially designated pigeon houses in which pigeons can nest, though how they explain this to the pigeons is anyone's guess.

But limiting our perceptions of pigeons to our own experiences is unfair both to the species and to us, as pigeons have actually done great things with their small selves. Take, for instance, the case of Cher Ami, a carrier pigeon in World War One. When a unit went far afield, its commander often carried several "war pigeons" along, and when he needed to relay a message back to headquarters, he would put it in a capsule attached to the bird's leg. Because of their ability to always find their way back home (believed to have something to do with Earth's magnetic field, though evidence suggests they may also use familiar landmarks), the pigeons would return to headquarters and trip a bell, letting the Signal Corps know a new message had arrived and also that there was probably now poop on their desks.

In 1918, during the Battle of the Argonne, a battalion of the 77th Infantry Division, commanded by Major Charles Whittlesey, found itself surrounded by Germans. In an effort to provide protection to Whittlesey's men, the Americans began firing artillery, which unfortunately fell on Whittlesey's position. Major Whittlesey affixed a message to the leg of his last pigeon, Cher Ami. It read: "We are along the road parallel to 276.4. Our own artillery is dropping a barrage directly on us. For heaven's sake, stop it."

As soon as Cher Ami took off, the Germans saw him and immediately opened fire. Cher Ami almost fell from the sky, but then pulled up and flew back to headquarters. The shelling stopped, eventually the Germans were forced to retreat, and the other survivors of what became known as the Lost Battalion were rescued. Cher Ami carried his message home despite having been hit in the breastbone, blinded in one eye, and having had the leg carrying the message nearly shot off (it was eventually amputated). For his intrepid service, the French awarded Cher Ami the *Croix de Guerre*, and General Pershing himself saw him off to America, where Cher Ami became a national icon. And once back in the U.S., his missing limb came in hugely handy for hitting people up for handouts.

"Tear me off a piece of pita bread?"

Thus does Cher Ami—and the numerous other pigeons who have served valiantly—remind us of the dangers of leaping to conclusions about entire groups. So next time a pigeon is hitting you up for a scrap of food or pooping on your shirt, think of Cher Ami, toss him some trail mix, and wear that bird poop proudly.

GRADE: B

WATER

BLUE WHALE

The blue whale (*Balaenoptera musculus,* lit. "What in the . . . ?") is, at nearly 200 tons, the largest animal that has ever existed.[1] Though such a massive creature is difficult to measure, the National Marine Mammal Laboratory has accurately weighed a female at 196 tons (392,000 pounds). Specimens over 200 tons[2] are believed to have been collected, though weighing anything this big is difficult when it's rapidly decomposing in your living room.

"All we have to do is find the volume of the ocean with the whale and subtract the volume of the ocean without the whale and multiply that by the density of . . . wait . . . never mind. Let's just guesstimate."

---

[1] Blue whales are bigger than the largest dinosaur, which capped out at one hundred tons. *Pffft.*

[2] To put this size in perspective, a two-hundred-ton blue whale weighs as much as two thousand fully grown Midwestern men. Or five thousand runway models. Or eighty thousand Chihuahuas.

The numbers on a blue whale[3] are truly staggering. At up to 108 feet in length, it has a lung capacity of over 1,320 gallons. Its flippers can be thirteen feet long. The tongue is three tons. A baby blue whale is born weighing three tons and can gain 200 pounds in a single day. The heart of a blue whale can be 2,000 pounds. The aorta is nine inches in diameter. It has *two* blowholes. Its hat size is 8.

"I had a puppy once, but it died."

The logistical numbers that support a single blue whale are equally mind-numbing. To feed, the blue whale opens its mouth and scoops in prey along with volumes of water. It then partly shuts its mouth and presses its tongue against its upper jaw, forcing the water to pass out sideways through the baleen plates, thus sieving out the prey, which is then swallowed. Each baleen plate is over three feet in length. In a given day, an adult blue whale will eat as many as forty million krill. Also in a given day, it will go through five thousand

---

[3] Their names notwithstanding, blue whales are actually usually gray on their upper sides, and the head and tail fluke are generally uniformly gray, while the flippers are rather mottled with dark blues, grays, and blacks. But they look bluish under water, and when you're rushing to come up with a name before anyone else can, you don't have time to dry off two hundred tons of *Balaenoptera musculus*.

pairs of socks, one thousand toothbrushes, and forty thousand bars of soap. A single pair of alligator-skin pants for a blue whale requires over eleven billion alligators and fifty million preteen Chinese sweatshop employees. Blue whales do not carpool.

Obviously, an animal of this size should stay in the water, where buoyancy can support it. The blue whale would make, for instance, a really terrible tree dweller. And it would be an atrocious bird of prey. And an utterly useless migratory animal of the grasslands.

Sadly, he never made it to the first watering hole.

Blue whales are usually in pods of two or three, but are also often found alone. This may or may not have anything to do with their melancholy underwater songs (which everyone of course pretends to like, because who has the courage to tell the largest animal in history that its songs are boring and somewhat derivative?). Regardless, blue whales like to be alone or with very small groups, because putting four or more blue whales in the same location could cause the ocean to break.

Blue whales are so big—and so fast (reaching speeds of up to thirty miles per hour, though they slow to barely three miles per hour when feeding)—that for many years they proved futilely difficult to hunt. But thankfully, in 1864, an enterprising Norwegian

"Even if I weren't a constitutionally reticent Scandinavian, I still wouldn't try to explain myself to a bunch of hippies in a dinghy."

by the name of Svend Foyn invented a steam-powered whaling ship with seven harpoon cannons that each fired a rocket harpoon *and* a grenade. Which put an end to *that* problem. Thus was the modern whaling industry inaugurated, and the population of wild blue whales (not including the ones in captivity, which has always been—and likely always will be—absolutely zero) fell below two thousand before whaling bans in the 1960s brought their numbers back, though it's still not anywhere near the hundreds of thousands that once roamed the seas. It is for this reason that Svend Foyn is almost never regarded as the spiritual grandfather of Greenpeace.

Still, today blue whales face the threat of periodically bumping into oceangoing vessels—collisions in which there are no winners. And while most other sea creatures would just as soon leave a two-hundred-ton whale alone, a pod of orcas pulled one of the great jerk moves of all time when it was seen attacking a blue whale, a behavior that almost outweighs the good work orcas do by hunting and eating great white sharks. But you take the good with the bad.

When grading an animal, many factors have to be considered, all with the goal of finding the appropriate balance that reflects the many plusses and minuses of the species at hand. But sometimes, one aspect outweighs all others, and in this case it's weight. When the animal in question is the largest thing that's ever lived on planet Earth, the choice is simple. Of course, our decision does not reflect the opinions of billions of krill (mostly dissenting).

GRADE: A+

GREAT WHITE SHARK

Even as the Discovery Channel tells us over and over that the great white shark is not a natural predator of man, the reality is that great whites account for more human fatalities annually than every other animal and nonanimal cause of death combined. Smoking, heart disease, cobra bites—these numbers pale next to the havoc wreaked by Nature's perfect killing machine (the great white shark).

CAUSES OF DEATH ANNUALLY, BY PERCENTAGE

- ■ GREAT WHITES
- ■ NOT GREAT WHITES

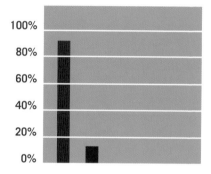

Teeth? Check. Jaw? Check. Cold, dead eyes? Double check.

Many misconceptions surround the great white shark (*Carcharodon carcharias*, trans. "The Banality of Evil"), and probably none is more inaccurate than the notion that they're not constantly trying to eat us at every opportunity, 24/7/365. Simply put, most of us will at some point in our lives be eaten by a great white shark. Those of us who aren't will know someone who is. Millions upon millions of people every year are eaten as the great white makes its way through the oceans in an unfettered bloodlust.

The great white shark (aka the white shark, white death, the devil's teeth, white pointer, el tiburon blanco, Weisshai, grand requin blanc, kelb al-bahr, simak al-qarsh al-abyud al-kbir, great white shark, white shark, white pointer, el tiburon blanco, great white shark, white shark, great white shark, white pointer, et cetera) is the largest predatory fish, holding the title of apex predator no matter where it roams (which is everywhere, with a large and deadly concentration in South Africa, Australia, California, and your bathtub).

"I have a pickup order for human flesh?"

Given how often they eat us, remarkably little is known about the great whites. They have never been filmed mating, for instance, because they have standing orders to eat people who film them doing anything. Nor is it clear why they swim across entire oceans pretty regularly, though, again, it probably has something to do with eating people. What is known is that the great white's skin can get a suntan. No kidding. It's important to look good while terrorizing bathers. They also have razor-sharp, serrated teeth in their massive mouths, which is their primary tool of attack (crossbow bolts rank second). They have five rows of teeth in various stages of development, the last two rows being completely unnecessary and entirely just for show. If one tooth falls out, another, larger tooth takes its place, and over the course of its life a great white will go through thousands of teeth. Eating people is hard work.

Now you're just asking for it.

Great whites can weigh as much as three thousand kilograms (three hundred thousand pounds) and be up to 6.4 meters (twelve hundred feet) in length. They can detect the smallest trace amounts of blood in the water, which is often an indication that there's something (or, as they prefer, someone) to eat nearby. We also know that great whites have ampullae of Lorenzini, which are a series of sensing organs that detect electromagnetic fields of potential prey. These can detect five billionths of a volt, which means that if you're within a mile and a half of a great white, it knows exactly where you are. To paraphrase Sarah Connor, everything about the great white is designed to make it a more effective Terminator.

"I have detailed files on human anatomy."

The one redeeming feature of the great white? Their lateral line system, which they use to detect vibrations in the water. Again, this makes them better hunters. Why exactly this makes for a redeeming quality, nobody knows. We're just really trying to find some positives here.

In the world of sharks, great whites are just *different*. They're the most terrifying, the most awful, the most hauntingly graceful. In 2004 the Monterey Bay Aquarium in California took possession of a baby great white that a fisherman caught in his net, apparently after being possessed of some kind of death wish. Watching even a five-foot great white prowling a massive tank, surrounded by other species of shark and fish, one could not help but stare in complete awe as its terrifying beauty emerged from the far shadows of the tank and passed the glass, unmolested in its role as Nature's perfect predator. It sailed along, like a bored airplane, strong, graceful, silent.

That very same shark later killed everyone at the zoo and escaped to Mexico.

The great white is one of two shark species[1] that can breach the water, which is a consequence both of its speed and of its interest in seeing if there's anything to eat in the air. Great whites have been known to take out low-flying 747s.

But still, no matter how much of its time the great white spends looking for people to eat (100 percent), for an animal that does one thing (hunting/killing), it does it really well. Perhaps a little *too* well. Or a lot too well, as in many ways the great white is a one-trick pony (but it's a *really* good trick). And instead of a pony, it's a deadly shark with no feelings.

One last thing you should know: Great whites make terrible pets. Just awful, awful pets.

GRADE: A+

 **FUN FACT** A mother killer whale's milk can be over 40 percent fat. But it's *so* delicious.

 **FUN FACT** The larger the animal, the slower the heartbeat. The blue whale's heart, for instance, beats once a year, on its birthday.

---

[1] The other is the mako shark, which is also the fastest shark, though only with respect to lateral forward motion, whereas the great white is the fastest eater.

SWORDFISH

The swordfish (*Xiphias gladius*, lit. "swordfish sword," which is confusing but leaves no doubt as to what you need to remember about the swordfish) is one of a small number of animals with swords on their faces.[1] Of these, they are by far the most massive, reaching almost fifteen feet in length (much of it sword) and one thousand pounds in weight (some of it sword).[2] They are also the sole member of family Xiphiidae; all the other members of the Xiphiidae family were found dead from sword wounds awhile back, and the police couldn't make anything stick on their main suspect (the swordfish).

A swordfish's nose sword isn't for decoration (though it certainly is a lovely nose sword). Instead, the nose sword is an important tool that is useful in a variety of situations, like a Swiss Army knife that's always open and has only a blade and no toothpick. The swordfish's

"NO COMMENT."

---

[1] Thankfully, the last swordcheetah was killed by former president Theodore Roosevelt in 1909 while on safari with his son Kermit.

[2] They are often confused with sailfish, which also have swords for noses, but if anyone ever tells you that they caught a sailfish, you should inform them that sailfish rarely weigh in at more than two hundred pounds and ten feet in length, and, you know, if they really wanted to go after something with a sword for a nose, they would have gone after a swordfish, but apparently they were too scared. (WARNING: They will probably then ask you to leave their daughter's quinceañera.)

nose sword literally cuts through the water, allowing the swordfish to easily reach speeds of fifty miles per hour (which is especially dangerous since they lack seat belts and they're waving a pointy sword). This speed, combined with their agility and nose sword, makes them deadly hunters. Contrary to popular belief, swordfish do not "spear" their prey; their hunting technique is to dart through schools of fish, slashing their sword noses around, hacking and/or stunning the confused fish who have never before seen a sword where a nose should be. On a given charge, a swordfish may feast on mackerel, bluefish, hake, herring, squid, giant drumsticks, mead, roast goose, suckling pig, jugs of wine, and sometimes their enemies' hearts—all the while surrounded by comely serving wenches. Oh, and their eyes and brains are heated (while the rest of them is cold-blooded), improving their vision dramatically and giving them a huge advantage over other fish in the sea. Anyway, the main thing is that eating with a swordfish is a bit of a grab bag, what with all the slashing and hacking.

The nose sword–aided speed makes swordfish largely invulnerable to predators. Since these fish are huge (and are equipped with huge nose

"Did you get my dinner-party evite? I'm slashing and hacking something special."

swords), the only animals that might reasonably make a go at them are killer whales, a few large sharks, and, to a lesser extent, grizzly bears. The short-fin mako shark is the rare animal fast enough to catch it, but that's clearly only half the battle when it comes to Sir Sword Nose. Head-to-head, a mako probably has only a slightly better chance of biting a swordfish with its mouthful of long, curved teeth before the swordfish runs it through the belly or gills, making Mako versus Swordfish (Quarrel in the Coral) *the* pay-per-view event of the year.[3]

"What say we leave the massive superfast fish with the sword on its face alone and go check out Magic Mountain?"

In sum, the swordfish is a really impressive animal. Why? Because it is a giant, fast fish that, in lieu of a nose, has a sword coming off its face.

Q.E.D.

GRADE: A-

[3] This is one reason why it's good to be human. We simply point at the leather-bound menu and the waiter says, *"Le swordfish soupe avec saffron rouille."* And we nod and that's all there is to it.

SEA CUCUMBER

The sea cucumber is the broad category for about twelve hundred echinoderm species within class Holothuroidea. Most inhabit the benthic zone of the world's oceans, scavenging detritus from the sea floor and eating tiny algae particles. Like all members of phylum Echinodermata, sea cucumbers have an endoskeleton just below the skin. Oh—and when threatened, many a sea cucumber will shoot its organs out of its anus. In shallow water, they can form dense populations and comprise most of an ecosystem's biomass. They sometimes send their own innards shooting out their anuses. The top skin covers microscopic pieces of skeleton called spicules. Just to make sure you got this, they defend themselves by defecating their own internal organs. And how they came up with this strategy is anyone's guess.

It's all you, dude.

Choosing to defecate its own organs as a defense technique is surprising and would appear, prima facie, to be much less useful than, say, actually *doing* something. Apparently the goal is to make a predator, no matter how famished, sick to its stomach and lose its appetite. Failing that, shooting its very own guts out of its very own anus is just so pathetic that even the hardest of predatory fish will give it an awkward pat on the back before making up an excuse to just get the hell out of there.

I'm gonna go.

Interestingly, the blood of sea cucumbers is yellow in color because as much as 10 percent of its blood-cell pigment is vanadium.[1] This was discovered when a scientist startled a sea cucumber and got an unexpected view of its entire insides.

Various sea cucumber species reproduce both sexually and asexually. However, given that its one and only trick is defecating its innards, we're guessing it's mostly asexual.

---

[1] Vanabins are a group of proteins that bind the metal vanadium; the few organisms that have vanabins in their blood are able to bind vanadium at levels one hundred times that of seawater. Currently it is a mystery as to exactly why sea cucumbers and other organisms collect vanadium. Another mystery is why sea cucumbers shoot their organs from their anuses.

As with all disgusting ocean creatures, the sea cucumber is considered a delicacy in Asia. And if you happen to get one that just shot its guts out its anus—well, you can imagine the excitement.

Oh, it's disgusting and horrible? I'll take three.

Basically, the sea cucumber digs around looking for dirt to eat, and when something bothers it, it shoots its guts out. It's like if you spent your life lying in the grass at a park looking for leftover chips to eat, and when the cops came to ask you what you were doing you promptly started kicking yourself in the crotch and vomiting up kidneys. Actually, that would probably work pretty well. But good luck finding work after that.

GRADE: D

SPOTLIGHT ON:
EXTINCTION

As we celebrate the animal species currently living (or in most cases, dwindling) on planet Earth, Animal Review would like to pause in remembrance of some of the precious ones we've lost over the last 3.5 billion years. We highly suggest playing "I'll Be Seeing You" as you read this list. You know, the one that goes: "In the morning sun and when the night is new / I'll be looking at the moon, but I'll be seeing you." Or whatever sad song you have around should work just fine.

In Loving Memory Of:

- The dodo
- The great auk
- Woolly mammoth
- American mastodon
- Saber-toothed tiger
- All of the dinosaurs
- Yunnan Lake newt
- Steller's sea cow
- Trilobite
- Passenger pigeon
- Passenger pigeon mite
- Acorn pearly mussel
- Dusky flying fox
- Broad-billed parrot
- Pig-footed bandicoot
- Long-tailed hopping mouse
- Tasmanian tiger
- Falkland Island wolf

To these and millions more: We miss you. Your memories will live on in our hearts and, in some cases, our biology books.

SPONGE

Sponges (phylum Porifera) are technically members of the animal kingdom. How exactly this is the case is, to the say the least, unclear. They lack tissues, muscles, nerves, and organs, and they feed by sitting there and waiting for nutrients to drift through their bodies.

Sure sounds like a plant, doesn't it?

Are our expectations now so low that we'll let *anything* into the animal kingdom with no questions asked?

This is nothing against sponges per se; the main problem with them is that there is no *there* there.

GRADE: D-

Meh.

CLAM

The clams fall under phylum Mollusca (aka "The Mollusks!"), class Bivalvia (aka "The Bivalves!") and have no head, no legs, no thumbs, and no anything very noteworthy, except a simple digestive tract and a small heart to power it (though via an open circulatory system, so let's not go nuts about that "heart"). In short, the clam is a mouth and an anus with a faint pulse that lives in a shell. Even so, many people like to pair clams with sauvignon blanc.

Phylum Mollusca, class Bivalvia, as viewed from the top of the food chain.

When they're not being delicious, clams serve a bigger purpose that often goes unnoticed. They give us perspective. There is one clam in particular that best illustrates this point. A clam named Ming. To understand Ming the Clam is to know all clams. Not that you really care to, but let's assume you do. And then we'll go from there.

Anyway.

The epic story of Ming the Clam ended abruptly in October

of 2007, when researchers working off the coast of Iceland found him in their dredge nets and estimated he was between 405 to 410 years of age, making Ming the Clam the oldest living creature ever discovered on earth.[1] This the researchers could tell only after they killed Ming and counted the growth rings on his shell. Science is funny sometimes.

In any event, this was one anus wrapped in calcium carbonate that had surely seen some things. In fact, Ming was alive toward the tail end of the Ming Dynasty in China (hence the name). He was around when the Mayflower landed at Plymouth Rock in 1620. Ming the Clam was here when Galileo Galilei peered into his telescope and said, "Uh . . . dudes? Somebody take the geocentric model out of the foyer." This clam witnessed the first spark of electricity, the birth of computers, and he was around when a crack team of American geeks put robots on the planet Mars and cried on television.

August 6, 1951. Ming takes a five-minute smoke break. Moments later, he returns to the sea and gets reprimanded.

---

[1] According to news reports, Ming was about thirty-one years older than the last animal thought to hold the world age record—another clam. Go figure.

While all of this madness was happening topside, Ming the Clam sat on the frigid ocean floor near Iceland, silently filter-feeding at his entry-level filtering job. He didn't have a desk, didn't get a paycheck. Nor did he take a day off to drive up to Santa Barbara for a long weekend. Nope, Ming just worked and worked and worked at the plankton, day in and day out.

Just imagine: four-hundred-plus years of going to work at a mindless filtering gig and never once getting any recognition whatsoever. Not even a certificate of merit, a most-improved trophy, Bivalve of the Month, or any of those acknowledgments that make you feel a little appreciated and, at the same time, a little sad to win them.

Without a word of encouragement, Ming filtered on for centuries. In the end, all he received for his years of grueling labor was a one-way ride to the surface and a fine welcome from a shucking tool on the deck of a filthy research vessel. As Ming would say, "Thanks for the memories."

The lesson in all of this is simple: Ming the Clam might never have come out of his shell (except when he was ripped from said

Not even a simple token of appreciation.

shell; see above), but even Ming's apparent life of thankless, unacknowledged duty can make us feel better about ourselves. For we, too, may be underappreciated at work. At times, we may even believe our careers are stagnant and devoid of meaning. But, thanks to clams and their extremely long life spans, we can at least take some comfort in the fact we won't be sitting in the same cubicle in the year 2398. Happy as a clam? Surely we can do better than that.

Clams should be rewarded for such a valuable demonstration. This added to the fact that they're quite tasty in garlic and butter earns them the acknowledgment they so desperately deserve—a passing grade. Congratulations, clams.

GRADE: C

➡ **FUN FACT** The giant squid has the largest eyes of any animal—they're up to twenty-eight centimeters across. That's over twenty-five centimeters!

➡ **FUN FACT** Kiwis have highly developed senses of smell and are the only birds with nostrils at the end of their noses. If you're ever in New Zealand, be sure to check that out. It's really something. Then you can leave.

SPOTLIGHT ON:
TAXONOMY

Taxonomy is the antiquated "science" of classifying organisms. It's helpful to think of taxonomists as the old librarians of the biology world. Although they don't much care if you open a noisy candy wrapper, taxonomists *do* get upset if you file a lemur under Monkey. Try that and you'll turn around to find a taxonomist glaring at you in disapproval, reading glasses dangling from a neck chain. Apparently, lemurs are prosimians.

Like the library, taxonomy is simply brutal if you don't understand it (and little help even if you do). This follows directly from the nature of taxonomy's abortively optimistic mission statement: to create an organized system for classifying the organisms of Earth. Right. Sure. Good luck with *that*.

As expected, the resultant hierarchical "system" is horrifying in its complexity. Taxonomy's basic categories (listed from top to bottom—getting more comprehensive as you move down) include domains, king-

Normal Person: "Hey, a tortoise."
Taxonomist: "Hey, a kingdom Animalia, phylum Chordata, class Reptilia, order Testudines, suborder Cryptodira, family Testudinidae, genus *Testudo* (disputed), species *T. horsfieldii*. Sorry. I couldn't help myself. I know, I'm the worst."

doms, phyla, classes, orders, families, genera, and species. Scattered throughout are suborders, superfamilies, and subspecies and other nonsense. And then there's the Latin. All animals are given a Latinate "binomial name" composed of the genus and species (e.g., you're a *Homo sapiens*[1]). Because otherwise, of course, anyone could understand what science is talking about and that's totally unacceptable.

One of the many mortal flaws of taxonomy is that it began in the eighteenth century when a Swedish guy named Carl Linnaeus started running around trying to group animals by physical similarities. The idea was love at first sight for scientists, and off they went, skipping and laughing, putting animals into categories according to appearances. Centuries (and many bloated categories) later, science invented DNA sequencing, which proved with complicated biochemistry once and for all that looks can be deceiving. Thus "Oops" became as common as "Good morning" among taxonomists, and their neat little system exploded into chaos. Thank you very much, deoxyribonucleic acid.

Today, taxonomy and many of its blunders have been woven into a new classification model called phylogenetic systematics, which is based on cladistics (the names tell you how much easier this stuff is). Basically, science is now considering the evolutionary context of a given animal—through fossil and DNA evidence—to "improve" classifications. But the new boss is just like the old boss. While more technically accurate, the modern system is replete with Latin and complicated hierarchical diagrams and surviving taxonomic structures. So, yeah, there's no way you're going to be close to ready for next week's midterm.

And for what? Animal-naming precision? Like we even need that. Hey, science, can't we just alphabetize everything (i.e., the lion is an *L* animal? Katydids are *K* animals? And flukes go under *F*?).[2] Then we can use all that extra time to look for near-Earth asteroids?

---

[1] Translation: "wise man." Yep. We love us.

[2] Or at the very least, just maybe classify everything under either Land, Sky, Water, or Other? It seems to be working pretty well here and nobody has *ever* complained about it being difficult to learn.

SALMON

Along with trout, chars, whitefish, and graylings, the salmon species are members of family Salmonidae (lit. "the rest of you are adopted"). Though closely related to trout, salmon are anadromous, meaning they live in saltwater but spawn in freshwater, while most trout lead comparatively residential life cycles in freshwater streams, as they just really hate to travel and, truth be told, consider *anything* that involves much movement to be nothing more than a huge hassle.

"I would love—just absolutely *love*—to come to your comedy show, but here's the thing . . . I kinda don't want to leave the house."

Much about the salmon remains unknown. It is unclear, for instance, how a smolt (an adolescent salmon, often derisively ridiculed as "Smolt the Dolt" and "Jerkface" by uncreative salmon upperclassmen) knows when to swim downstream and into the open ocean in preparation for adulthood. (Since they travel to the sea in large schools, it is likely that peer pressure plays some kind of role for the males, and, for the females, it probably has something to do with wanting to meet more mature males who don't do everything out of peer pressure.) Nor is it known how, after a few years in the open sea, salmon manage to return to their exact place of birth to spawn, though it is thought to have to do with Earth's magnetic field (a fairly common explanation for animal behaviors, such as pigeons' homing ability), their keen senses of smell, and the fact that more and more of them are getting GPS installed.

It is this annual migration—"the salmon run"—that stands as a tribute to the supremacy and the stupidity of Nature's grand *telos*. From the standpoint of evolutionary biology, a species exists only to reproduce. Not to learn guitar, not to memorize favorite lines of movie dialogue, not to get really good at badminton—but simply to exist long enough to make *more*. Though all species (except the panda) take this seriously, it is the salmon that has taken it to completely irrational heights, coming up with a bizarrely complicated mating plan that involves a great likelihood of being eaten by grizzly bears.

"I'm almost there, I'm almost there, I'm almost . . . hey, is that a bear?"

Long before they even get a chance at avoiding the jaws of *Ursus arctos horribili*s, a salmon with a yen to do some spawning has already moved into *casa loca*. They completely change colors, taking on

"WHO WANTS
TO DO SOME
MATIN'? OOPS.
SORRY, DUDE."

bright hues to better attract mates (or bears), and the males typically develop back humps and hooked mouths (called kypes) full of angry canine teeth. And as they begin their long journey the wrong way up a river, they stop eating.[1]

The salmon will swim—and swim and swim—sometimes up to several hundred miles—to spawn at the place they were born.[2] The entire way, the crazy-looking male salmon lays it on really thick to impress the ladies, acting aggressively toward anything that comes near them. This is, of course, a boon for fishermen, once again calling into question the whole let's-swim-upriver-for-hundreds-of-miles-while-I-act-crazy mating plan.

When (and if) they get to the place they were born, the female chooses a spot of gravel and cleans it with her tail to form a spawning bed, called a *redd* (by humans; salmon call it a spawning bed). The female then releases her eggs as the male releases his *milt* (or sperm, though salmon call it milt). Fertilization occurs in the water, and the female sweeps her tail to cover the eggs with gravel.

Then, after doing that a few more times, they die.

Having exhausted themselves with the journey up the river, and having not eaten the whole time, the salmon simply collapses.[3] And thus is the salmon the perfect example of how Nature plays her tricks. If the Chinooks just took a small step back, they'd realize that they're much better off staying put in the ocean, playing online video games with their friends, and eating too much fast food while watching *The Shield* on DVD. But because of how deeply Nature plants the desire to reproduce, they find themselves swimming thousands of

---

[1] Now *there's* some planning for you.

[2] They already know (from experience) that it's a good spawning site, though they sometimes get lost and end up at a new spawning site, thus maintaining the genetic diversity of the species. This change in scenery arises when a salmon loses patience with a GPS system that is always "recalculating."

[3] All species of Pacific salmon die after mating. Some Atlantic salmon will make it back to the ocean and be able to spawn again, though it's pretty hard to convince them they want to go through that again.

miles without food, acting stupidly to impress women, and hoping to avoid being eaten en route to dropping dead.

That was worth it.

But not only do salmon show how Nature uses irrationality in pursuit of a rational goal—they also show the dangers of appearing too useful to humanity. Salmon flesh contains a rich supply of omega-3 fatty acids, which anyone who has ever been condemned to a conversation with a Whole Foods employee knows is *the* key to health.[4] With alleged benefits ranging from the ability to prevent cancer, lower blood pressure, avert strokes, boost immunity, ward off depression, remove tattoos, teach you to read Arabic, and get your boss fired, the popularity of omega-3 fatty acids has begotten its own rich supply of faddish supplement sales. Overfished, collapsing oceans and indecisive health data be damned—we're getting ourselves some fish oil![5]

---

[4] Though depending on the aisle you're in, the key to health can also be açaí juice, Kombucha teas, and organic radishes.

[5] There are, of course, other sources of the exact same omega-3 fatty acid. Algae is one. Sardines, which reproduce quickly and whose supply is not threatened, are another. But who wants to eat sardines at a business lunch? *Precisely.*

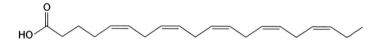

You can see the long carbon chain that can serve as the hydrophobic region of a cell membrane, and the carbon-carbon double bonds that would hypothetically serve to maintain membrane fluidity. But you already knew that.

The value of eating omega-3 fatty acids supposedly flows from their role in modulating internal inflammation responses, as well as from the fact that the body preferentially incorporates their long carbon chains into the phospholipid bilayer of the cell membrane. Whether and how important this is remains murky, however.

The salmon offers us a living, underwater-breathing monument to the irrational behaviors Nature burns into our souls, both to reproduce at whatever cost and to pay lots of money for whatever the bearded guy at the overpriced grocery store says is good for us.

And for that, we owe them (the salmon, not beard guy) a large debt of gratitude.

GRADE: B+

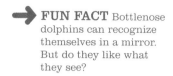

FUN FACT Bottlenose dolphins can recognize themselves in a mirror. But do they like what they see?

OCTOPUS

Why no superhero has adopted the octopus as an identity is a profound mystery.[1] With eight arms, surprising intelligence, and a host of phenomenal offensive and defensive capabilities, there is almost nothing this cephalopod cannot do. Yet everyone's still slipping into spandex unitards and naming themselves after bats, spiders, iron, and cats. There's even a guy called the Green Lantern—because if a city is being ransacked by maniacal criminals, the one thing the citizenry can really use more than anything in that situation is a lantern.

Throughout the world's oceans there are about 250 known species of octopuses (believe it or not, this is the plural form preferred by marine biologists over "octopi"—so have fun pedantically correcting everyone before taking a long draw on your mahogany calabash pipe). Pick one of these 250-odd species at random and you will find yourself staring down a skill set that reads like the Super Friends PowerPoint presentation. Octopuses are simply awesome, constantly surprising us with an arsenal of very real, scientifically confirmed powers. Best of all, there is still much that remains unknown about them—and it is precisely this "unknown" factor that would strike fear into the hearts of criminals and general ne'er-do-wells everywhere.

As everybody knows, octopuses have eight arms lined with rows of powerful suction cups. This is an excellent start for a proposed Octopus Man, but it's not enough—above all else, a superhero needs

---

[1] In fairness, there is a villain named Doctor Octopus who is always giving Spider-Man a hard time, but he's still way off the mark. For one thing, he has *four* robotic arms. Now, had he called himself Doctor Quadrilateral and showed up with eight arms, everyone would have laughed him right out of town. So what's the difference? To make matters worse, this so-called Doctor Octopus is a rigidly spined vertebrate who can't even escape through tiny spaces, nor spray ink in people's faces, nor camouflage himself while riding on a biological water-jet engine. Quite frankly, it looks like Dr. Octopus sketched his whole villain persona on the back of a cocktail napkin and then brought it to a metal-casting plant and said, "Build this." Anyway, the point is that the octopus superhero concept is still there for the taking, and also that doctorate programs are certainly not what they used to be.

"OH, RIGHT, HE'S GOT
A MAGIC RING. I'M
SURE THAT'LL BE A
BIG HELP."

smarts. Had Superman been of below-average intelligence, he would probably have just found himself making minimum wage as a flying X-ray machine doing outpatient work for an HMO (assuming malpractice insurance wasn't prohibitively expensive). Likewise, a dumb and frequently lost Wonder Woman piloting an invisible plane would have been a PR disaster for the feminist movement, not to mention a subject of great concern for both the FAA and air travelers.

"Not her again. She's going to kill us all."

Rest assured, then: The octopus is smart. This was officially realized in the 1950s, when an Oxford biologist trained octopuses to touch specific shapes to receive food rewards. It's also been demonstrated that they can open locked aquarium latches, remove the twist-off lid from a glass jar to obtain food, disable aquarium lights they find bothersome, quickly find the most efficient route through a maze, and then actually *remember* what they learned. This not only means that the octopus is the smartest of the invertebrates—it also means that Octopus Man is probably much more capable at tackling the rising tide of cyber-crime than either Hulk or Thor.

Not only would Octopus Man be spineless (but don't tell him that), he'd actually have no bones at all[2]—his beak and teeth would be the only hard parts of his body. On paper this appears problematic, but Octopus Man holds the huge advantage of being able to squeeze through incredibly small spaces to, say, hide inside a soda can (just like a real octopus) or slip beneath a blast door at a compromised bioweapons facility to take out a gang of terrorists (also just like a real octopus), who in the movie rewrite would be changed to rich and mysterious neo-Nazis in order to avoid offending anyone (except neo-Nazis with money).

Also important to the character of Octopus Man is the fact that octopuses are true masters of disguise. Their skin contains special cells called chromatophores, each of which has three sacs of pigment. By manipulating the size of each sac, they can alter the color that

"Wherever criminality lurks, wherever injustice lives, Octopus Man will be . . . wait, am I purple right now?"

---

[2] Some people may find it difficult to believe that Octopus Man could even stand up without bones, let alone disarm a missile filled with nerve gas. Well, he *can*.

emanates from each *individual* cell. The net result is that octopuses produce millions of subtle color variations, allowing them to blend into their surroundings in fractions of seconds. In other words, Octopus Man would be able to disappear in broad daylight, and, as a consequence, concealing his true identity by morphing into a newspaper reporter would be child's play.

The list goes on. Octopuses can eject a cloud of black ink to confuse predators or archnemeses. They can move with tremendous bursts of speed on a stream of water emitted from a biological jet engine. They have three hearts and blue blood, making them difficult to kill but aesthetically interesting to wound in the climactic battle scene. Plus their arms can regenerate, so the big fight scene at the end should *definitely* involve swordplay.

Finally, there's the recent finding that all octopuses are venomous.[3] Toxic saliva is the kind of discovery that just leaves the criminal mind racing with the fear of what could be next. Heat vision? ESP? The Sucker of Truth? Perfect pitch?

Who knows?

One note, however: Someone should probably tell our love interest about Octopus Man's toxic saliva. And with eight arms, he'd probably be kind of grabby.

But otherwise this one is a no-brainer.

GRADE: A

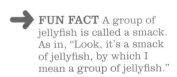

FUN FACT A group of jellyfish is called a smack. As in, "Look, it's a smack of jellyfish, by which I mean a group of jellyfish."

---

[3] Certain species more than others—the blue-ringed octopus has venom that can kill a human, while other octopuses can merely paralyze a clam. Which is still pretty cool. Unless you're a clam. Or an archvillain named The Clam.

OTHER

HIPPOPOTAMUS

The common hippopotamus is a massive sub-Saharan semiaquatic mammal of the family Hippopotamidae whose closest relatives are the whales and porpoises, though to be honest they hardly keep in touch anymore. The name for this largely vegetarian animal comes from the Greek words *hippos*, meaning "horse," and *potamus*, meaning "river," which yields "horse river" and gives a pretty good indication as to why people stopped learning Greek. The hippo is identified by its barrel-shaped torso, enormous head, hairless body, and stubby legs, as well as by obviously being a hippo.

More than any other animal, the hippopotamus manages to combine adorable comedy value with sheer terror. Unlike the lions, tigers, bears, cobras, and great white sharks—all of whom *look* like animals that will kill you—the hippo is bald and fat. Instead of fear, your first impulse upon seeing one is to dress it in a tutu and invite it to perform at your kid's birthday party. But as too many people have found out the hard way, this is a very bad idea that will ruin almost

So I shouldn't try to put a red bandana and tiny cowboy hat on them?

LET'S TALK
ABOUT YOUR
PARENTS.

any get-together.[1] For their adorableness obscures the fact that hippos are killers. In so many words, in Kingdom Animalia hippos are the guy in his mid-forties who lives alone and juggles his time between his jobs of part-time party clown and full-time serial killer.

As with human serial killers, hippos usually seem harmless and can be remarkably charming, yet won't miss a chance to bite you in half with their massive tusks. Also like human serial killers, precise statistics on how many victims they've killed are unavailable, though, again, some experts believe them to be the world's deadliest animal. And as with human serial killers, hippos don't actually float, but instead run and paddle along the bottoms of lakes and rivers while holding their breath for up to five minutes, and then try to capsize boats of sightseers.[2] However, unlike human serial killers, they can also hear underwater, so don't gossip about them while they're down there because they're totally listening and will then turn it around and guilt you into letting them kill you.

He always kept to himself.

---

[1] Unless it's an animal-murder theme party, in which case it's a great call.

[2] Steve Irwin, who used to make a joke of dangling his own babies in front of crocodiles, once said that taking a boat across a river filled with hippos was the most dangerous thing he had ever done.

Whatever you do, don't look behind you or you'll fall over laughing and be killed instantly.

Before giving in to your burning desire to hug a hippopotamus and put lipstick on it and try to see if you can ride it, consider these facts: A male hippo can weigh up to eight thousand pounds and be fifteen feet in length, while their two-foot-tusk-filled mouths can crash down with several thousand pounds of pressure when these fiercely territorial animals feel like defending their space, which is always.[3] Also consider that hippos live in groups of up to forty called a *pod*, *herd*, *dale*, or *bloat*. This part is less important, though.

Nature was clearly messing with us when she made hippos so profoundly cute. The massive head, the pear-shaped body, the stumpy limbs—everything about a hippo begs us to feed them treats and knit them whimsical little sweaters. And if you've ever seen a hippo lumbering over land at up to thirty miles per hour, well, you've known pure bliss. Just don't try to get them to play fetch.

The obvious temptation toward failing the hippopotamus (for

---

[3] For a sense of how territorial hippos are, go to a zoo and toss a melon into their pool. Every hippo will immediately charge with rage in its eyes and hate in its heart until realizing that it's a yummy melon. The reaction is easily worth the hassle and weirdness of smuggling a melon into a zoo. Or so we're told.

being so darn cute to the extent that we have to constantly remind ourselves how they are waiting to kill us) is assuaged by a few factors. First, hippos have been known to bite crocodiles in half, and in this regard they're sort of like a serial killer who kills bad people, though, unlike Dexter, they're more than happy to kill you, too, because you happened to wander past. Second, they spin their tails while defecating to cover the greatest possible area with dung and better mark their apparently never-ending territory. And third, they are retromingent, meaning that they urinate backwards, likely for the same reason. And you have to give credit where it's due.

GRADE: D

FUN FACT Crocodiles cannot stick out their tongues. And if they could, they wouldn't anyway.

FUN FACT If you have to write an animal report for class, pick the black-crowned Central American squirrel monkey. It's endangered. But more important, if you use its common name ten times, that's sixty words right there.

GOLDEN DART FROG

We all remember the classic children's fable in which a princess kisses a golden dart frog and, while she waits for it to transform into a handsome prince, her heart begins to flutter, and eventually she realizes it's not a good flutter at all but really a very serious ventricular fibrillation induced by a potent neuro/cardio toxin. Then she immediately falls over, dead.

The moral of the story, of course, is that you should never, ever touch—let alone make out with—an extremely poisonous amphibian. Especially the golden dart frog (*Phyllobates terribilis*, lit. "terribly embarrassing death by frog"). It's estimated that of the 180 known species of dart frogs indigenous to Central and South America, all of which are poisonous to varying degrees, the golden dart frog of Colombia is far and away the most lethal. It is, by many accounts, the most toxic animal on this planet and single-handedly accounts for Colombia's shamefully high PMR (Princess Mortality Rate).

"Can I turn into a handsome prince? Maybe I can, maybe I can't. Why don't you come over here and kiss me and we'll find out together."

If the scientific name *P. terribilis* and the fact that it's an evil yellow frog aren't enough to deter oral contact, then perhaps some sobering biochemistry will. When disturbed, the golden dart frog secretes a ghastly powerful alkaloid batrachotoxin—from glands on its back and behind its ears—with the chemical formula $C_{32}H_{42}N_2O_6$ and a molecular mass of 538.67 g mol^{-1}.

But no need to concern yourself with the technical stuff. All you really need to know is that this organic molecule acts specifically on voltage-gated sodium channels by increasing the permeability of sodium cations, which in turn irreversibly depolarizes the cell membranes that the Na^+ channels serve, effectively blocking neuro-muscular transmissions,[1] which is an obvious problem when it comes time to oh, say, live and breathe and the like. Indeed, the entire mechanism is remarkably simple:

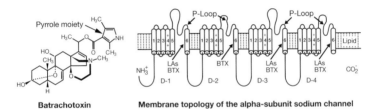

Batrachotoxin Membrane topology of the alpha-subunit sodium channel

See there? You learn something new every day.

In short, if the frog's alkaloid batrachotoxin finds its way into an animal's bloodstream (via a minuscule cut on your hands, for instance), it will completely shut down the peripheral nervous system *and* lead to cardiac arrest. One frog carries enough toxin to kill one hundred people, so obviously it doesn't take much to kill one. You could probably hide a lethal dose of the golden dart frog's poison under a couple grains of sand.[2] Stated in less engaging scientific terms, a

---

[1] Discussion question: Sodium ion channels are also present in the nerve and muscle cells of the golden dart frog. So why does it not succumb to its own toxin? (The answer is upside-down at the bottom of this page. Nah, we're just messing with you. The frog evolved sodium ion channels that aren't affected by the alkaloid batrachotoxin.)

mere one hundred micrograms in the bloodstream will kill someone who weighs 150 pounds. If you want to kill someone who weighs 96 pounds or 223 pounds or some nonmultiple/divisor of 150, or a European who reports his weight in kilograms, you'll have to set up the stoichiometric equations yourself.[3]

Dart frogs are so named because Amerindians in Central and South America's rain forests are famous for using their toxins on the tips of blow darts. They catch the frog, hassle it, and then proceed to rub their darts all over the frog's backside (which, by this time, is just absolutely *glistening* with death). Thus armed, they head out into the jungle, load the blowpipe, and recite the warrior's creed of "Dude. *Seriously*. Be *really*, *really* careful where you point that thing." (This is a good time to remind *The Animal Review* readers that one should never eat a monkey dispatched by a Colombian Amerindian. It's supposedly safe to digest the golden dart frog's toxin after it's been cycled through an animal, but better to be safe than sorry. Stick with the plantains.)

By now you've most likely heard enough and, if you're like most people, you definitely want a golden dart frog for the terrarium in your living room. This is dumb but, sadly, doable. Dart frogs raised in captivity do not produce the alkaloid batrachotoxin, because this ability is entirely diet-dependent. It was recently discovered that the golden dart frog feeds on a beetle that gorges itself on poisonous plants. The beetle accumulates the toxin and posthumously passes it up the food chain to the dart frog. If denied these insects, golden dart frogs will eventually lose their toxicity. But this process may take years, so the wild-harvested golden dart frog is recommended only for that special kind of weirdo hobbyist who doesn't mind a very real risk of killing the cat, the maid, the neighbors, the neighbors' kids, his or her kids, his or her frog-curious friends and loving parents, the landlord, the cable guy, the phone guy, the TV repairman, and/or him/herself.

---

[2] But that would be weird.

[3] It is beyond boring. We don't want to know about it. Just keep your units straight and that's all we have to say on the matter.

"Do I still secrete a deadly neuro/cardio toxin? Maybe I do, maybe I don't. Why don't you try cleaning this terrarium and we'll find out together."

Be that as it may, the innocuous-looking but deadly golden dart frog is headed toward an excellent mark. Animal Review is more than willing to award an A to any animal that can instantly kill whatever eats/kisses/touches it, out of awe of Mother Nature (and also fear). However, there is a snake called *Liophis epinephelus* that has somehow developed immunity to the golden dart frog's poisonous wares, and so the golden dart frog is regularly reminded that DNA mutation is a double-edged sword.

GRADE: A-

➡ **FUN FACT** The female golden orb weaver spider produces silk that's five times stronger than steel by weight. And no ego. It's refreshing.

PEACOCK

Most animals lead lives of quiet desperation, humbly eking out a living and doing everything they can to avoid calling attention to themselves long enough to reproduce before being eaten by wolves or, more likely, before a hunter decides that they'd make a nice-looking hat.

You know what I think would really be cool? A hat made from those animals that break into our garbage.

Not so the peacock. While sharing membership in family Phasianidae (lit. "Guess who the family star is?") with pheasants, grouse, and chickens, the peacock stood out from a young age in ways that the chickens, quite honestly, resented a great deal. Because peacocks, unlike most other animals, hold *nothing* back. Loud, bold, pushy, impossible to ignore—the peacock is truly That Guy of Kingdom Animalia.

How cocky are peacocks? Cocky enough that they are all known to most people as peacocks, even though only the males are peacocks; the females are peahens, whom everyone likes more than the peacocks. But they're not free of blame for the peacocks' awful personalities, as they choose mates based on the color and size of the male's plumage, encouraging peacocks to appear as ridiculous as possible in order to attract a harem of several peahens. Peacocks are also cocky enough that a group of peafowl is known as a party, a designation chosen after the peacock kept insisting that if he was

"SORRY I'M LATE, MY FLIGHT WAS DELAYED COMING BACK FROM MILAN FASHION WEEK. BUT LET'S LIGHT THE CANDLE ON THIS LITTLE SHINDIG. DID I TELL YOU ABOUT THE TIME I HAD DINNER AT BONO'S HOUSE?"

there, "then it's definitely gonna be a party," and everyone agreed to it just to get him to shut up.

There are two main species of peacock. The Indian peafowl is native to the Indian subcontinent and is revered there for its ability to absolutely suck the air out of any room. By way of contrast, the green peafowl inhabits a range from Burma to Java, where it is known by its incessant need to challenge everyone to push-up contests. There is also the rare white peafowl, which also breeds in India. Suffice it to say, his personality wears on you like sand in a swimsuit.

"Careful, I don't want to get smudged. I probably shouldn't sit down. Can you bring me some scotch? I'll tell you about how good scotch is made when you get back. Thanks."

Dealing with a peacock is, unsurprisingly, fairly awful. They have been kept as pets for thousands of years, giving humans plenty of time to hear every single one of their grating stories about how awesome they are at French cooking and Muay Thai. They're quite testy, though, and don't mix well with other animals (especially when one of them has the temerity to ask if it's even possible to bungee jump out of a moving Cessna at thirteen thousand feet).

Peafowl can fly, albeit short distances, mostly to get into trees

for the night. They don't *like* to fly, however, because it's less time that they can spend talking about themselves. They are omnivorous, enjoying a diet of ticks, termites, ants, mice, flower petals, and minnows, and will try just about anything simply for the sake of being able to talk about it later. They possess sharp, powerful metatarsal spurs that they can use to protect themselves, and they also like to tell everyone how they're expert marksmen. Of course, their most notable characteristic is their utter lack of self-awareness.

When all is said and done, peafowl are precisely what their common name suggests: an unbearable group of animals with few real friends, screwed-up personal relationships, and a high likelihood of being cast on a reality show.

GRADE: D

FUN FACT The cheetah can run at speeds of up to about seventy miles per hour. The ostrich can run around forty miles per hour, but it usually makes up ground in the cycling leg of the triathlon.

SPOTLIGHT ON:
ANIMAL SOUNDS

One would tend to believe that sounds sound the same to everyone, irrespective of native tongue. That explosions sound like explosions, screeching car tires like screeching car tires, and other parts of action movie set pieces like other parts of action movie set pieces. However, one would be wrong. Or perhaps all sounds *do* sound the same, but how they get processed in foreign brains and repackaged into onomatopoeic words varies widely.

This is true of animal sounds as well. For instance, English speakers describe a cat's purr as *purr*. French people describe the same sound as *ronron*. Likewise, for an English speaker, bees buzz, but to a Japanese person, they "boon." To Germans, they "summ." And whereas Anglophones think a pig sound is *oink*, Germans think the pig noise is *grunz*. Russians think pigeons make a "guli-guli" sound, and to Hungarians it's "burukk."

The list goes on. To Greek ears, a turkey doesn't say "gobble gobble"—it's saying "glou glou." In English, a lone wolf's howl is *Owoooo*. In Swedish, it's *Oooahh*. (Okay, that's not *that* different, but they ought to know better.)

And then there are the roosters. English people imitate a cock crowing as "Cock-a-doodle-doo." But Danes say "Kykyliky." Italians, "Chicchirichi." Finns, "Kukko kiekuu." And in Turkish, roosters go "Oo-oore-oo."

Who's right and who's wrong is beside the point—what's important is that everyone get on the same page, and fast. Why? Absolutely no reason at all.

But seriously—let's figure this out.

Fast.

CAPYBARA

The South American capybara, *Hydrochoerus hydrochaeris*, is the world's largest living rodent. It can weigh up to 140 pounds, but what's really interesting is that it bears a striking resemblance to Mr. Spock from *Star Trek*.

"I also get Natalie Portman a lot."

Luckily for everyone involved, capybaras are herbivores, a fact that offsets the discomfort with both their size and their genetic ties to the rodentia crime family. Plus, the really horrifyingly large rodents are long gone: In early 2008 the BBC, fresh out of news, reported that a fossilized skull belonging to *Josephoartigasia monesi* (two to four million years old, give or take a few minutes) was recently found in Uruguay. Some scientists estimate this rodent species would likely have been about five feet tall, ten feet long, and weighed up to 2,200 pounds. Some other scientists speculate

"Howdy, ma'am. You have a what now?"

that it probably also had atrocious gas. Long story short, good luck getting a dead one of those out of your storm drain.

But *J. monesi* is long since extinct (thank you, saber-toothed tiger) leaving the capybara as the poor man's freakishly large rodent.

Today, capybaras can be found in the wild throughout most of the South American continent, where they spend their days annoying the daylights out of ranchers with their competitive grazing.

When capybaras aren't being nuisances, their skin makes nice leather and their meat apparently resembles pork. If you need any other reason to see one (you really don't), they also have webbed feet that allow them to swim like the dickens, and they can hold their breath for five minutes (give or take two million years). This is why, in South America, they say, "Check your pool before you go swimming, because there might be a capybara in there holding its breath, waiting to scare you." This sounds much more profound in Spanish.

As for the name *capybara*, it comes from Guarani, a language of indigenous people in South America. It means "master of the grasses," which does little to dispel the stereotype that indigenous people tend to overstate things. Meanwhile, the capybara's Greek name, *Hydrochoerus hydrochaeris*, means "water hog." Guess which nomenclature scheme these animals prefer.

Let's skip gestation periods and social interaction and say this: The capybara deserves a little credit for refusing to scurry into the trash can when people turn on the lights. Instead, at 140 pounds of rodent, the capybara has really embraced the whole being-a-rat thing. If criminals followed their lead, we'd have much less crime. What's more, they're not ashamed to do their Mr. Spock impression.

GRADE: B-

→ **FUN FACT** The most massive insect ever recorded (as far as we know) was New Zealand's giant weta, which weighed in at seventy-one grams (.16 pounds). But rest assured, scientists are spending tons of federal grant money looking for heavier ones.

LADYBUG

Of the roughly 350,000 species of described beetles, and the estimated one to eight million undescribed beetle species, the ladybug (family Coccinellidae, lit. "nature's homecoming queen") is the only one who can land/crawl on or near a human being without risking severe bodily injury or death. Even among the simplest members of Kingdom Animalia there are advantages to being attractive.

"I got pulled over for speeding once . . . the officer gave me a warning and then asked for my phone number."

In America and in parts of Northern Europe, tradition holds that a ladybug landing on one's body brings good luck and makes wishes come true as the person fortunate enough to be graced with the ladybug's presence gently releases it to the wind. Contrast this with, say, the also-harmless-but-horned rhinoceros beetle, whose impromptu appearance on a shirt sleeve is generally greeted with gasps, followed by exaggerated attempts to remove it and then murder it where it falls. Things are so much easier when you're pretty.

As one might expect, the ladybug's cosmopolitan grace and classical good looks have a positive effect on everything in her life. Not only is she never bothered with things like getting squashed under a boot heel, she also enjoys regular free meals. Because ladybugs are cute *and* they eat aphids (aka destructive "plant lice"), many gardeners love having them around to be cute and eat aphids. Who needs skills? Similarly, the Mall of America, a megamall in Bloomington, Minnesota, has released, over the years, more than one million ladybugs in its indoor park as a natural form of pest control. The mall also gets the ladybugs whatever they want at Ann Taylor.

"I'm not even allowed in the Gap."

With respect to their sanguine coloring, it should be noted that ladybugs are in possession of some smarts, too. Stick with us here. The ladybug is poisonous—she can emit a yellow alkaloid toxin from her joints that goes with her outfit and is, while noxious to her natural nemeses, mostly harmless to humans and other large animals who tend to adore her and thus overlook things like yellow alkaloid toxins secreted from arthropod joints.

But rather than proving this toxicity posthumously (i.e. after being eaten), she simply advertises the fact by being seen around town in bright-red designer wings—a visual cue for "Don't even think about biting me, you loser." In other words, she's broadcasting the message that she's literally drop-dead gorgeous. Or at minimum, drop-dead unpleasant to take a bite out of.

Biologists call this colorful warning strategy aposematism. The idea is that a given predator eats one brightly hued/toxic animal, gets sick, and the next time it spots the same creature it thinks: "Oh, yeah. *That* thing." As this translates for the ladybug, life becomes less about kicking off her high heels and running away from small birds and more about rosebush hopping and fun and calling her friends from backstage at the Dave Matthews concert and saying, "Trish, you are *not* gonna believe this . . ." And so forth.

"Have I showed you this picture of me already? I did? Sorry. I was just checking to see if I showed you this picture of me already."

It turns out aposematic coloring works out well for both predator and prey, because each avoids harm with very little effort. Though nothing in the aposematism playbook says adorable and complementary colors are required. This is clearly the ladybug's personal take on the whole thing. But it suits her, and serves as yet another reminder for the rest of us that cute pays in dividends.

Especially when the grades come in. As the ladybug always says after she's had a few too many margaritas at the Mall of America food court, "It's like . . . it's like . . . don't hate tha playa, hate tha game, because, like, some people? Sometimes don't like me becauthe I'm pretty and stufff." Then she almost passes out and we all rush over to make sure she's okay.

GRADE: A–

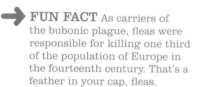

FUN FACT As carriers of the bubonic plague, fleas were responsible for killing one third of the population of Europe in the fourteenth century. That's a feather in your cap, fleas.

REPORT CARD

KING COBRA: A+
BLUE WHALE: A+
GREAT WHITE SHARK: A+
SKUNK: A
OCTOPUS: A
VULTURE: A-
SWORDFISH: A-
GOLDEN DART FROG: A-
LADYBUG: A-

NORTH AMERICAN MOUNTAIN GOAT: B+/A-
BULLET ANT: B+
OWL: B+
SALMON: B+
WILDEBEEST: B
PIGEON: B
CAPYBARA: B-

BALD EAGLE: C+
CLAM: C
KOALA: C-

GIRAFFE: D
SEA CUCUMBER: D
HIPPOPOTAMUS: D
PEACOCK: D
GARDEN SNAIL: D-
SPONGE: D-

PANDA: F
ALPACA: F
LOCUST: F

PHOTOGRAPHY/ ART CREDITS

- Amanda Chou: Sea cucumbers in bowl (Sea Cucumber)
- Anthony D. Kitchens: Sea cucumber with ejected guts (Sea Cucumber)
- Bernd Reinhardt: Exterminator man (Capybara), roommate (Vulture)
- Burton Wright Jr.: Bullet ant on leaf (Bullet Ant)
- Charles Hotham: Hippo chasing man (Hippo)
  Ed. note: For the record, the park ranger in the picture narrowly escaped with his life and later testified against the hippo in court.
- Devin Edmonds: Both golden dart frogs (Golden Dart Frog)
- Erik K. Veland: Baby koala in tree (Koala)
- Jonne Roriz: Satere-Mawe tribe ritual (Bullet Ant)
- KC Slagle: Photoshop of war-hero pigeon Cher Ami (Pigeon), locust life cycle (Locust), batrachotoxin structure (Golden Dart Frog), omega-3 fatty acid structure (Salmon)
- Marc Montocchio/SeaPics.com: Original photo of schooling fish with marlin, which was altered to look like a swordfish (Swordfish)
- Patrick Phegley: Clam thank-you mug on desk (Clam)
- Phillip Colla: First sea cucumber (Sea Cucumber), surfacing blue whale (Blue Whale)
- Richard Herrmann/SeaPics.com: First swordfish (Swordfish)
- Ron Dunnington: Markhor goat (North American Mountain Goat)
- Ryan Faught: Svend Foyn drawing (Blue Whale), yeti drawing (North American Mountain Goat)
- Scott Sandars: Pigeon coop (Pigeon)
- Sharon See: Photoshop work on swordfish with schooling fish (Swordfish)
- William Dutfield: Beware-of-hippo sign (Hippo)

ACKNOWLEDGMENTS

Animal Review thanks all the people whose help, encouragement, and expertise made this book possible (in alphabetical order by first name):

Andrea Morrison, Ben Adams, Bernd Reinhardt, Bob Malone, Bob Morrison, Brent Butler, Carrie Majer, Cory Evens, Craig Powell, David Oshinsky, Elizabeth Van Itallie, Gerald Nash, Hannah Gordon, Jeff Berger, Jon Schroeder, Karen Nash, KC Slagle, Ken Crosby, Kendra Coggin, Laura Phillips, Nanci Richardson, Nick Trautwein, Nicole Lanctot, Patrick Phegley, Peter McGuigan, Rebecca Costell, Rebecca Lentz, Rodney Munoz, Ryan Faught, Ryan Reeves, Sharon See, Shirin Nash, Steve O'Donnell, Suzie Parkinson, Ursula Lentz, Will Georgantas

Also: the writers and staff at Pajiba.com and EDSBS.com. Great sites, all.

A NOTE ON THE AUTHORS

JACOB LENTZ has written for *Jimmy Kimmel Live* since the show's debut in 2003. A former editor of the *Harvard Lampoon*, he is the author of *Electing Jesse Ventura* and coauthor of *There's No I in Office: 4293 Meaningless Phrases to Keep Your Coworkers Smiling While Avoiding Actual Conversation*. In his free time he enjoys thinking about animals and looking for opportunities to nap.

STEVE NASH has spent the last fifteen years as a writer in advertising, working for numerous Fortune 500 companies. A recovering pre-med student with a background in science, he also has a degree in psychology from the University of California at Santa Barbara. His favorite book is *Electromagnetic and Optical Pulse Propagation 2: Temporal Pulse Dynamics in Dispersive, Attenuative Media*.

For more information, click here.